NO MORE ANXIETY!

NO MORE ANXIETY!

Be Your Own Anxiety Coach

Gladeana McMahon

KARNAC
LONDON   NEW YORK

First published in 2005 by
H. Karnac (Books) Ltd.
6 Pembroke Buildings, London NW10 6RE

British Library Cataloguing in Publication Data

A C.I.P. for this book is available from the British Library

ISBN: 1 88575 381 2

Edited, designed and produced by The Studio Publishing Services Ltd, Exeter EX4 8JN

Printed in Great Britain by Hobbs the Printers Ltd, Totton, Hampshire

Contents

ABOUT THE AUTHOR   xi

INTRODUCTION   1
- What's special about a cognitive–behavioural   1
  approach?

HOW WILL THIS BOOK HELP ME?   3

WHAT IS ANXIETY?   4
- Too much of a good thing – the stress response   4
- Are some people more susceptible?   6
- Could I have learnt to be anxious?   10

DIFFERENT TYPES OF ANXIETY   12
- Generalized anxiety disorder (GAD)   12
- Obsessive compulsive disorder (OCD)   12
- Hypochondriasis   12
- Post traumatic stress disorder (PTSD)   13
- Phobias   14
- Social phobia   14
- Panic disorder   14
- Burn-out   15

FREQUENTLY ASKED QUESTIONS   16
- Can my anxiety harm me?   16
- Will I have a nervous breakdown?   16
- Why do I feel so tired?   16
- Would resting be better for me?   16
- Can I really learn to control my anxiety?   17
- What about medication – isn't there a
  pill that will cure me?   17

Contents

BECOMING ANXIETY FREE   18
- Help yourself manage stress   18
- Techniques and strategies for managing stress   18

ANXIETY-FREE THINKING   26
- The four stages of change   26
- Does optimism pay?   27
- Are my thoughts real?   29
- Faulty thinking   31
- Healthy thinking   32
- Negative thoughts   33
- Types of negative thinking   33
- Edit your thoughts   41
- Challenge your thoughts   43
- Demands that may increase your anxiety   48
- Challenging your demands   49
- Summary   52
- Learn to accept yourself   52
- Tips to help you like yourself   53
- Learn to appreciate yourself   57
- The life audit   57
- Distraction   59

ANXIETY-FREE EMOTIONS   60
- Learn to be emotionally smart   60
- Learning to appreciate yourself and others   64
- Other people's emotions   65
- How to deal with strong emotion   66
- Cost–benefit analysis   70
- The role of assertiveness   71
- Shame and humiliation   72
- How to deal with shame and humiliation   73
- Dealing with worry   73
- How to worry constructively   74

● Relaxation 75
● Hyperventilation 76
● How to use coping imagery to deal with 77
negative emotions

ANXIETY-FREE ACTIONS 80
● Graded exposure 80
● Panic attacks 82
● Using coping imagery to reduce anxiety 84
● Medication 86
● Problem-solving 87
● Assertion training 95
● Assertiveness quiz 95
● Four types of behaviour 96
● What assertiveness involves 100
● Some assertiveness skills 102
● Managing instant reactions 103
● Less is more 103
● More assertiveness skills 103
● Your personal rights 106
● Dealing with difficult situations 108
● Dealing with requests 109
● Handling criticism 111
● Giving criticism 111
● Managing put-downs 112

WHAT AN ANXIETY-FREE LIFE REQUIRES 114
● Time management 114
● Stress busting 120

THE ANXIETY-FREE DIET 123
● Anxiety and dietary tips 123
● What can I do to help myself? 124
● What food can I eat? 126

Contents

WHAT TYPE OF HELP IS AVAILABLE?   128

- ● Talking about the problem   128
- ● Self-help groups   128
- ● Learning to relax   128
- ● Psychotherapy   129
- ● Medication   129

FURTHER READING   130

USEFUL RESOURCES   131

CONTACT ME   142

INDEX   143

To Mike
Thank you for always being there for me

About the author

The *Independent on Sunday* listed Gladeana McMahon as one of the UK's top ten coaches. She combines academic rigour with down-to-earth communication skills and has provided therapy and coaching to politicians, celebrities, senior business people, and those in the media.

A Fellow and Vice President of the Association for Coaching, she holds Fellowships with the British Association for Counselling and Psychotherapy (BACP), the Royal Society of Arts (RSA), and the Institute of Management Studies (IMS). She is a BACP Senior Registered Practitioner, Accredited Counsellor and Supervisor and a BABCP Accredited Cognitive–Behavioural Psychotherapist who is United Kingdom Council for Psychotherapy (UKCP) and United Kingdom Register of Counsellors (UKRC) registered. She is also a Certified Neurolinguistic Programming (NLP) Coach and NLP Master Practitioner.

Gladeana is Co-Director of the Centre for Stress Management and Centre for Coaching and is an Honorary Visiting Lecturer in the Psychology Department of the University of East London where she taught on the Diploma and Masters' programmes for many years.

An internationally published author, she has written, edited or contributed to over twenty books on a range of subjects and continues to edit a number of professional journals. Her media work includes being co-presenter of *Sex and Soaps*, a five part series for Granada Television, psychological adviser, guest counsellor and co-presenter for BBC1's 25-part series *Life's too Short* and resident counsellor for Channel 5's *Espresso*. She has appeared on shows such as *Celebrity Wrestling – bring it on!*, *Strictly Come Dancing Takes Two*, *Britain's Worst* and *Richard and Judy*. Gladeana is life coach for GMTV and stress coach for Channel 4 Websites and has acted as psychological adviser to shows such as *Extreme Celebrity Detox*, *Desperately Seeking Sheila*, *Brat Camp*, *Bad Lads Army*, *Model Behaviour*, *The Club*, *Home Alone 14*, *Shattered*, *Fashanu's Football Challenge*, *Melting Pot* and *Big Brother*. She was Talk Sport's Life Coach and agony aunt for *YES Magazine* and currently writes a regular Life Coaching column for the Women's Section of the *Daily Express*.

INTRODUCTION

What's special about a cognitive–behavioural approach?

The problem with using words like counselling or psychotherapy is that these words suggest there is only one method of therapy. However, at the last count there were some 450 different therapeutic approaches, some sharing ideas in common and others being as different as chalk and cheese.

Cognitive-Behaviour Therapy is a relatively new therapy. Behaviour Therapy came first in the mid-1950s, aimed at helping people deal with the symptoms of anxiety by changing the things that they did. Although Behaviour Therapy was a movement forward as it provided many people with real benefits, it also became apparent that something was lacking, and this turned out to be the attention to the person's individual thoughts that accompanied his or her behaviour.

In the late 1960s, Cognitive Therapy came into being and this therapy focused on the types of thinking styles that caused people distress. It was not long before the benefits of Behaviour and Cognitive Therapy came together, forming what is now called Cognitive–Behaviour Therapy – often referred to as CBT. Cognitive–Behaviour Therapy is the only therapy that has sought to put itself forward for assessment and validation through research, its practitioners believing it important that a therapy should not only work but should demonstrate how it works and why. There are now many studies supporting the view that the best treatment for a range of conditions is CBT and, indeed, the National Institute for Clinical Excellence (NICE) and the National Health Service (NHS) have both recommended CBT as the treatment of choice when working with conditions such as depression and anxiety.

HOW WILL THIS BOOK HELP ME?

This book takes the skills and techniques of CBT and offers you the opportunity of taking control of your anxiety. It aims to help you understand what is happening to you and teach you how you can overcome your fears. If you use the skills outlined in this book you will learn how to become your own anxiety coach.

Some of you may find it helpful to read the book through once before returning to do the exercises. Others may find it more helpful to tackle each of the exercises as they come up. It's up to you to decide which method suits you best.

For some people, using the skills in this book may be enough to achieve freedom from anxiety. For others, the book will help to reduce the anxiety they experience. For a few of you this book may make little difference at all. If you are in this last group don't see this as a failure on your part but rather as an indication that you require specialist help and need to see a Cognitive–Behaviour Therapist.

WHAT IS ANXIETY?

Too much of a good thing – the stress response

Fear can be a good thing. For example, if I go to cross the road and see a car speeding towards me, I would experience all the physical and emotional sensations of anxiety. However, if I felt the same way waiting for a bus when there was nothing to fear, this would not be a helpful or appropriate response. Fear is a crucial survival mechanism and our bodies are pre-programmed to protect us from dangerous situations.

Biologically, our bodies produce a range of stress hormones, such as adrenaline, that encourage changes in our physical and mental state, helping us either to escape from the situation or face it head-on. This is called the 'stress response' and you may have heard it called 'fight or flight'. The three key players when it comes to stress hormones are adrenaline (associated with flight), noradrenaline (associated with fight), and cortisol.

When we experience this type of reaction we often feel muscle tension, increased heart rate, breathing and blood pressure. We may sweat and experience changes in our digestive system such as feelings of "butterflies" in the stomach. Our thinking may become more focused on the task ahead and we may be able to do things that we would not normally be able to. You may have heard stories of people who have undertaken superhuman feats to save a loved one – for example, a child is trapped under a car and a parent is able to lift the car to save the child.

There is a third response that can be triggered and this is the 'freeze' response, where the person stops and becomes very still. Although this is a less common response, it can be very effective in the right circumstances – for example, if you were hiding from an attacker.

Like anything in life, too much of a good thing can become a problem. The stress response is essential, and yet for many it has become a burden rather than a blessing.

(Figure 1 shows you what happens to your body when it experiences the stress response.)

The stress response is only meant for short-term use, so if it is not switched off when the danger passes a number

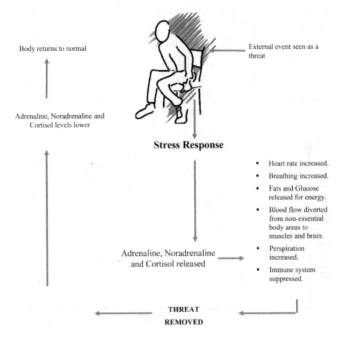

Body returns to normal

External event seen as a threat

Adrenaline, Noradrenaline and Cortisol levels lower

Stress Response

- Heart rate increased.
- Breathing increased.
- Fats and Glucose released for energy.
- Blood flow diverted from non-essential body areas to muscles and brain.
- Perspiration increased.
- Immune system suppressed.

Adrenaline, Noradrenaline and Cortisol released

THREAT REMOVED

Figure 1.   The stress response.

of problems can occur and our ability to cope lessens, as shown in Figure 2.

The physical, mental and behavioural sensations associated with 'fight or flight' that are essential for managing crisis situations turn into something quite different when the stress response is not turned off. A list of symptoms is outlined in Table 1.

Are some people more susceptible?

The Office for National Statistics (ONS) states that one in six adults suffer from some kind of mental distress while another major study quotes one in four. According to the ONS, around three in ten people in the UK experience some type of mental health issue. Combined anxiety and depression affects 9.2% of people, generalized anxiety disorder 4.7%, phobias 1.0%, obsessive compulsive disorder 1.2% and panic disorder 0.7%. As you can see,

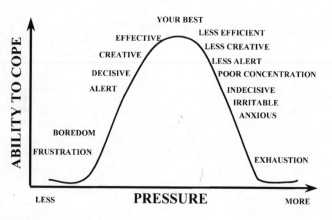

Figure 2.   Personal performance levels

6

Table 1. Symptoms of anxiety

Physical signs	Emotional signs
Tightness in chest	Mood swings
Chest pain and/or palpitations	Feeling anxious/worrying more
Indigestion	Feeling tense
Breathlessness	Feeling angry
Nausea	Feeling guilty
Muscle twitches	Feelings of shame
Aches and pains	Having no enthusiasm
Headaches	Becoming more cynical
Skin conditions	Feeling out of control
Recurrence of previous	Feeling helpless
illnesses/allergies	Decrease in confidence/
Constipation/diarrhoea	self-esteem
Weight loss or weight gain	Poor concentration
Change in menstrual	
cycle for women	
Fainting	
Tiredness	

Behaviour	Thoughts/psychological aspects
Drop in work performance	"I am a failure'
More inclined to become	'I should be able to cope'
accident-prone	
Drinking and smoking more	'Why is everyone getting at me?'
Overeating/loss of appetite	'No one understands'
Change in sleeping patterns	'I don't know what to do'
Poor time management	'I can't cope'
Too busy to relax	Loss of judgement
Stuttering	Withdrawing from family and friends
Loss of interest in sex	Poor judgement
Inability to express feelings,	A sense of being on a kind of 'automatic pilot'
Emotional outbursts and	
over-reactions	
Nervous habits such as	
drumming fingers	

anxiety-related conditions affect many people. You are not alone!

There are a number of factors associated with anxiety-related conditions. These are family history, stressful life events, thinking style, poor coping skills, individual personality and lack of social support.

Family history

Research has shown that conditions like anxiety and depression often run in families. As yet, no one really knows how much this is due to genetic influences and how much to learning anxiety-type behaviours and thinking style from family members. Even if you are born into a family that is predisposed to anxiety, it does not automatically mean that you cannot overcome the condition if you develop it. Much of our behaviour is learnt and, if a behaviour or way of thinking can be learnt, it can be unlearnt and new behaviours developed if the individual is prepared to put some work in.

Stressful life events

Everyone experiences stressful periods from time to time. Sometimes these events take the form of bereavement, job loss, or relationship problems. Any event where we feel threatened is likely to spark off feelings of fear and anxiety. Psychologists discovered that even pleasant experiences such as having a child or gaining a promotion could be stressful as they also contain change; too much change, even positive change, requires a degree of emotional re-adjustment.

Thinking style

People who think in certain ways are more likely to feel

anxious. Such thinking styles include the ability to discount the positive (always putting down or dismissing anything positive that is said) or maximizing negative events by being overly pessimistic and dramatic. There will be more about this type of negative thinking and the relevant antidotes later in this book. Research has shown that there is a strong link between what you think and the mood you feel. The more negative the thinking the more anxious a person is likely to feel, particularly when the thoughts are based on perceptions of threat. For example, someone may have taken out a large mortgage, have a baby on the way and then discover there is a strong likelihood of being made redundant. If an individual's thinking style is adaptive and healthy he or she may feel worried, but if it is pessimistic, severe anxiety is a more likely outcome.

Poor coping skills

Many of us have some excellent coping skills that we can call on when we need them. For example, you may have learnt that dealing with things that need to be done rather than worrying about them decreases your feelings of anxiety. However, most of us have some coping strategies that are unhelpful such as drinking, smoking, or eating too much as a way of comforting ourselves.

Individual personality

Your basic personality type is likely either to help or hinder you when it comes to dealing with stress and anxiety. In the late 1960s, cardiologists discovered what have come to be known as Type A and Type B personalities and, more recently, a third has been added called the

Hardy Personality. Type As are ambitious, competitive, hard-driving and more likely to ignore stress symptoms. They tend to go down rather spectacularly when they become overloaded. Type Bs are more laid-back and find it easier to keep matters in perspective, whereas the Hardy Personality seems to have all the attributes of a Type A but without the susceptibility to stress.

Social support

Over the years research has demonstrated that people with good support systems in the form of family and friends are far more likely to ward off the effects of trauma. The more people we have to talk to the more we are protected from the full effect of dealing with stress on our own. A lack of a social network really shows itself in times of crisis.

Could I have learnt to be anxious?

It is certainly possible that you could have learnt to become anxious. If one of your parents was so timid that every time you went to try something new as a child he or she would seem scared and tell you to stop, you would learn that life is not safe. After all, as a child, our parents are the people we look up to and learn from. In certain situations you would have learned not to take risks or to overcome obstacles and are therefore more likely to develop an anxious approach to life.

It might be helpful to think of childhood as a type of training course where those who look after us are the trainers. If the trainers are well trained and able to pass on the life skills needed we will go on to develop these skills. However, if through no fault of the trainers they do not have the skills or are going through a bad time that stops them from being able to pass on the skills, then it is likely we will not develop the skills we need.

DIFFERENT TYPES OF ANXIETY

Generalized anxiety disorder (GAD)

People who suffer with this form of anxiety feel worried all the time about almost everything. Many people describe it as a feeling of being tense, restless, or on edge. GAD sufferers interpret many ordinary situations as threatening in some way. Symptoms include trembling, feeling shaky, headaches, muscle tension or aching, especially around the neck and head, feeling hyped up, restless, getting tired easily, difficulty in sleeping, problems with concentration, irritability, forgetfulness, and many of the symptoms outlined in the stress response.

Obsessive compulsive disorder (OCD)

People who suffer from OCD describe feeling a compulsive urge to take part in ritualized activities: for example, checking locks and gas taps many times before being able to leave the house, washing hands or clothes excessively or engaging in excessive cleaning. These behaviours are often accompanied with repetitive actions like having to check the gas taps in a certain way and for a certain number of times. If something happens to break this routine, the sufferer has to start the ritual all over again.

Hypochondriasis

Sufferers from this disorder are plagued by health fears, being convinced, regardless of how many medical tests are

12

made or reassurances given, that they are really ill. For example, someone believes that the normal aches and pains experienced by most people at some time are due to cancer and so enters into a cycle of medical test after medical test, going from one doctor to another, never being convinced that all is well.

Whether relating to OCD or hypochondriasis there is usually a set pattern of reactions:

1. The perceived threat triggers a worrying thought or image and this leads to a feeling of anxiety.
2. The person then needs to engage in an activity that he or she finds comforting (e.g., washing hands, checking etc.) to reduce the feelings of anxiety.

Post traumatic stress disorder (PTSD)

Post traumatic stress is often experienced following what is often termed a traumatic incident. A traumatic incident is one where the person was involved in or witnessed an event that involved serious threat of death to a loved one or self. PTSD often happens when a person feels intense fear, helplessness, or a sense of horror. For many people the feelings following a traumatic event pass within the first 4–6 weeks, often without any help. However, for some, the feelings do not pass and may even get worse, and their sense of fear leads them to avoid people, places and things that remind them of the event. In addition, people may also experience "flashbacks" of some aspect of the traumatic event. It is not unusual for people with PTSD to suffer from other anxiety conditions.

Phobias

People experiencing phobias have an extreme fear of something specific. For example, common phobias include fear of dogs, cats, spiders, water, heights, small places, open spaces, blood, thunder, etc. The fear experienced can be extreme and may severely limit an individual's ability to function. A person may develop agoraphobia, finding that over a period of time they become fearful of open spaces and welcome the safety feelings that certain places offer. Phobias are often accompanied by panic attacks, as listed below.

Social phobia

Some people experience a different type of phobia: that of social phobia. People with this condition fear being with others and may avoid being around people or being seen eating in public or being in any situation where the person feels he or she is going to be evaluated in any way.

Panic disorder

Panic disorder is another way of describing a condition where people experience repeated panic attacks. Someone experiencing a panic attack will experience a period of intense fear with a range of accompanying sensations. These sensations include: pounding heart, trembling, shortness of breath, a choking feeling, chest pain, nausea, dizziness, a sense of not feeling real, fears of going crazy or of dying. A few people may experience only one or two panic attacks. Others may have such attacks on a daily basis, varying in intensity from mild to severe. Women are twice as likely to suffer than men and panic disorder often starts in late adolescence or early adulthood; research tends to suggest that the condition can be genetically inherited.

Burn-out

Burn-out is the term used to describe someone who is suffering from extreme stress that tends to be built up over a period of time. As you will be aware from the stress response discussed earlier, when we perceive a threat we produce stress hormones to deal with the situation. If a person finds him or herself exposed to stressful life situations for a prolonged period of time burn-out can occur. One of the common symptoms associated with this condition is anxiety.

FREQUENTLY ASKED QUESTIONS

Can my anxiety harm me?

You will have heard the expression that he or she "died of fright". Although this statement is used to illustrate a point graphically it is not, thankfully, true. No one can die from anxiety or fright. Anxiety is a really uncomfortable feeling with physical side effects, but that is all.

Will I have a nervous breakdown?

Anxiety does not cause problems like nervous breakdowns. Many people who suffer from mental illness may feel anxious but anxiety itself does not cause mental illness.

Why do I feel so tired?

Anxiety is a tiring emotion to experience. Your body is working hard producing and coping with a range of stress hormones and their effects. It is hard to cope with life when you are anxious. Once you are able to manage your anxiety you have more energy.

Would resting be better for me?

You might feel that resting is better for you and it is true that you need to use your energy wisely. However, anxious people often avoid situations and then find reasons to justify their avoidance behaviour. In fact, avoidance only makes anxiety worse, while learning to deal with it diminishes and then eliminates the problem.

Can I really learn to control my anxiety?

Yes, it is possible to learn to control your anxiety and even to eradicate it. Once you have practised your anxiety management techniques you will gain more control over your feelings, your body and your life.

What about medication – isn't there a pill that will cure me?

Medication can be of help. However, medication will not cure the problem but will simply mask it. The only real way to deal with your anxiety effectively and in the long term is to learn to live your life differently. The problem with medication is that you end up having to take more and more and the effects wear off more quickly.

BECOMING ANXIETY FREE

Help yourself to manage stress

Help yourself by remembering that you can always take *some action* to minimize, even if only by a small amount, the stress you experience.

Come to your own aid by:

A anticipating stressful activities and planning for them.
I identifying the major sources of stress in your life.
D developing a range of coping strategies that you can use on a regular basis so you become familiar with them and can call upon them when you really need them.

Techniques and strategies for managing stress

You can choose from the following range of techniques to suit your own preferences and circumstances.

Use your support systems

Maintain or establish a strong support network. Come to terms with your feelings and share them with others. Ask for help when you need it and accept it when it is offered. You can always offer help to other people when you are stronger and they need it. For now, it's your turn to accept help.

Relaxation

Relaxation can also play an important part in dealing with

stress and in managing anxiety. Simple ways in which you can find time for yourself are:

● Take time to enjoy a bath, light some candles, sprinkle a few drops of lavender aromatherapy oil into the water and play some gentle music while you take time for yourself.
● Dim the lights in the lounge, play some gentle music, close your eyes and allow yourself time to relax.
● Take some time to enjoy your garden or local park. Take time to look at all the trees and flowers.

Relaxation exercises

There are many forms of relaxation exercises, ranging from those that require physical exertion or movement to those that require nothing more than breathing or visualization techniques. Listed below are three common relaxation techniques.

Breathing

● Breathe in through your nose for a count of four;
● Breathe out through your mouth for a count of five;
● As you breathe out, consciously relax your shoulders.

As you breathe in and out, use your stomach muscles to control your breathing. For example, when breathing in use your stomach muscles to push out and when you breathe out use your stomach muscles to push in. This way you will breathe more deeply and this will help you gain the maximum benefit from this kind of relaxation.

When people are anxious they tend to breathe shallowly. When this happens the body gets less oxygen and many people are therefore tempted to breathe faster to make up for this deficit. However, breathing too fast can make a person feel dizzy or faint and may be frightening. This type of breathing can lead to a condition called hyperventilation that is described more fully on page 78.

Keep practising the above until you feel confident that you would be able to undertake this breathing exercise anywhere and at any time. It is simple but effective, and can take the edge off feelings of nervousness. It is particularly helpful for times when you are about to face up to a difficult situation or a confrontation.

Muscle tensing exercise

1. Lie on the floor and make yourself comfortable.
2. Starting with your feet, tense all your muscles and then relax them. Focus on how heavy your feet feel and the way in which they are sinking into the floor.
3. Tense all the muscles in your legs as hard as you possibly can, then relax them. Focus on how heavy your legs feel and the way in which they are sinking into the floor.
4. Move up along through the other parts of your body – hips, stomach, chest, arms, neck and face – tensing and relaxing the muscles as you go.

Note: If you suffer from high blood pressure or heart problems, you should consult your doctor before engaging in this particular exercise.

Visualization

1. Choose a safe place to sit or lie down.
2. Imagine you are in a garden at the time of the year

you like best, enjoying looking at flowers, shrubs, trees and so on.

3. You notice a wall along one side of the garden. In the middle of the wall is an old fashioned wooden door with a wrought iron handle on it.

4. You make your way over to the door and open it.

5. On the other side, you find yourself in your own, very special, safe place. A place no one knows about and where no one can get you.

6. Enjoy being there.

7. When you are ready, make your way back to the door.

8. Leave and shut the door firmly behind you, knowing that your special safe place is always there, whenever you choose to return there.

9. Walk around the garden and, when you are ready, open your eyes.

Note: This exercise can take between two minutes and half an hour, depending on how much time you wish to allocate to it.

Anchoring

'Anchoring' is a simple technique whereby you associate positive, calming, confident feelings to a particular object, usually, but not always, something you wear frequently. All that's required is that in moments of anxiety you touch the chosen object and then focus on the feelings associated with it.

1. Choose an object, say, a ring.

2. Now, close your eyes and focus on some aspect of your life that brings a warm glow or a smile to your

face. This could be a person, place or an activity that makes you feel good about yourself.

3. Rub the ring as you reflect on that happy thought and continue doing so for five or more minutes.

4. Wait for a few minutes and then repeat the process.

5. In carrying out this simple routine, you will have anchored positive feelings to your chosen object. From now on, merely touching that object should bring on good feelings instantly.

Anxiety and dietary tips

Anxiety can be made worse by taking stimulants such as tea, coffee, colas and chocolate, all of which contain caffeine. Caffeine is a stimulant and stimulants are best avoided when we are experiencing emotions such as anxiety and anger. Because we produce adrenaline when we are feeling anxious, this can affect our blood sugar levels and they may indeed drop dramatically. Therefore, in order to keep those levels balanced, it is important to eat 'little and often' during the day. It may also be helpful to avoid refined sugars and other substances that give too much of 'a high' too quickly. Slow-release foods such as carbohydrates (potatoes, pasta, rice, bread, apples, and bananas) are a much better idea as they fuel the body in a more even, controlled way.

Managing your time

Time is a valuable commodity as there is only so much of it, and learning to manage your time effectively will certainly reduce your stress levels. As Time Management is an important skill to understand and learn to do well a whole section has been dedicated to this subject on pages 114–120.

Sleep

It is important for a person's psychological and physiological well-being to get adequate sleep. Sleep is essential for survival, health and fitness and research suggests that it is the quality of sleep that is most important. However, too little or too much may lead to poor performance. The amount of sleep required varies considerably from person to person. Most people sleep seven hours; some may need nine and others only five. Ironically, it is often the worry about losing sleep that produces more negative symptoms than the loss of sleep itself. Many people underestimate the amount of sleep they actually get due to the amount of time they spend worrying about not sleeping when they are awake.

The kind of sleep that is most important is what is called REM, or rapid eye movement, linked to dreaming. All people dream even if they wake without any memory of dreaming.

Stress is one of the main causes of sleep disturbance. Many people lie awake at night worrying about problems or thinking about the future in an anxious manner; then having finally fallen asleep awake feeling tired as the original worries are still there.

If you are experiencing difficulties sleeping it can help to:

- Ensure you have a routine. Have a warm milky drink as milk contains tryptophan, which promotes sleep.
- Take a warm bath. Using relaxing bath oils may also help.
- Avoid sleeping during the day.

- Avoid drinking caffeine as caffeine is a stimulant and may keep you awake. Too much coffee during the day could still affect you in the evening.
- Avoid a heavy meal and eating late at night.
- Ensure you get plenty of exercise during the day. It may be particularly helpful to take your exercise during the late afternoon or early evening.
- Use your relaxation exercises as outlined above.
- Ensure your sleeping environment is as pleasant as possible, not too hot or too cold. Switch off electrical appliances to avoid a 'mains hum'.
- Turn the clock away from you. Research has shown that turning the clock away from you helps if you are having problems sleeping as clock watching is liable to keep you awake, whereas not knowing what the time is encourages you to sleep more.

If you are not sleeping because of a traumatic event, you may also need to feel secure in your sleeping space. For example, ensure that all doors and windows have proper locks and are alarmed.

Some people find that changing the position of the bed or rearranging the layout of the bedroom can be helpful, as can removing objects such as pictures or ornaments that may seem frightening in a half-awake state. Introducing pleasant smells may also create a pleasant atmosphere. Lavender oil is particularly popular and recommended by complementary health practitioners such as aromatherapists to aid relaxation and sleep.

If you find yourself unable to sleep within forty-five minutes of going to bed, then get up and engage in another activity such as reading. After 20–25 minutes go back to bed again and try to get some sleep. Repeat the process if you still have not fallen asleep for as long as is necessary. It is important your bed remains associated with sleeping.

People may experience nightmares following a traumatic incident. If this is the case it can be helpful to:

- Write down the dream in the third person (*John could not breathe*), then in the first person (*I could not breathe*), until you feel more comfortable with the dream.
- Think about what the dream might mean. Is it an actual replay rather like a flashback of the traumatic incident, or is the dream completely different?
- Think about how you could change the story. For example, if you were trapped, perhaps you could find a way out or a sudden surge of strength to remove the item trapping you. Practise this new version of the dream in your imagination while you are awake.
- When you have practised your new version of the dream then practise it again when you are tired and relaxed and before going to sleep.
- Tell yourself that you intend to replace the dream with the new ending the next time it happens.

You may find you have to repeat this exercise before it becomes fully effective. It would be helpful to keep a note using the 0–8 scale of the distress experienced of each nightmare. You may find that if the nightmares do not stop they may change in degrees of severity, and by keeping a note of this, you can see how your nightmares are weakening.

ANXIETY-FREE THINKING

The four stages of change

Whenever you learn something new, regardless of whether it is a practical skill like using the Internet or a mental skill such as changing behaviour or negative beliefs, you go through a set sequence of learning, as follows:

Stage 1	Stage 2	Stage 3	Stage 4
Unconsciously incompetent	Consciously incompetent	Consciously competent	Unconsciously competent

This process is known as Robinson's Four Stages of Learning.

Stage 1: unconsciously incompetent

'*Don't know it and can't do it.*'
    You feel unhappy but have no idea why.

Stage 2: consciously incompetent

'*I begin to notice just how often I have negative thoughts but I don't seem able to change anything.*'
    During this stage you become aware of what is happening but seem unable to do anything about it. This is the awareness stage: for example, realizing the ways in which you make yourself feel anxious by seeing everything in all-or-nothing terms but not being able to stop.

Stage 3: consciously competent

'*I have skills and can handle situations better although I still have to think about what I am doing.*'

You now have a range of strategies to use but you still have to think about what you are doing as it does not feel natural.

Stage 4: unconsciously competent

'*I suddenly realized what I had done and how I handled the situation without even thinking about it.*'

The more you practise your new skills the more your behaviour feels 'natural'. You are now working off your automatic pilot – doing things without thinking about them.

Change happens over time and it is persistence, practice and the belief in taking one small step at a time that wins the day.

Does optimism pay?

Optimists think more positively about life, seeing the good in situations and minimizing the bad. Pessimists think that optimists are foolish and optimists think that pessimists are depressing. Researchers believe that optimism and pessimism have a genetic factor. However, there is also evidence to suggest that it is the environment we are brought up in that shapes the way we think. We discussed earlier in the book the way that behaviours can be learned, and this is true for optimists and pessimists.

There is research to suggest that there are advantages to being an optimist. For example, it would appear that optimists live longer, achieve more and have happier lives.

When you suffer from anxiety, it can be hard to believe that you can ever become more optimistic about life. However, it is possible to relearn behaviours and ways of thinking. The following exercise will help you begin this process.

EXERCISE

Situations where you experience optimism and pessimism

1. In a notebook, write down the names of two people you feel more optimistic around and state why.
2. Identify two situations that you have felt more optimistic about and state why.
3. Name two people you feel pessimistic around and state why.
4. Identify two recent situations where you have felt pessimistic and state why.

When you look at your answers can you spot any patterns forming? For example, are you more optimistic with certain people but pessimistic with others?

Pessimism drains you. However, pessimistic thinking can be changed. Changing your thinking style is perfectly possible if you are prepared to put in some time and effort.

A third group has been identified: those who plan for the worst or devise a fall-back position if things don't work out as hoped. They never believe anything good will automatically happen. However, they do put themselves forward even though they do not believe they will succeed. They work hard and prepare. These are called 'Defensive Pessimists'. Defensive pessimism seems to work for some people. If you have a go you are probably a defensive pessimist – if you don't you are a pessimist.

The following exercise is aimed at helping you begin the process of increasing your optimistic outlook on life.

EXERCISE

Ways of improving optimism

(a) Make a list of three good things that have happened to you at the end of each day. The things you list do not have to be major items but simply tasks you may feel you have handled better than you thought you would.

(b) When you find yourself looking at life pessimistically replace your negative thought with a positive thought or image.

(c) Make a list of positive statements and repeat these to yourself on a daily basis (e.g., '*I am able to conquer my anxiety*'; '*I can learn to think and behave differently*').

Are my thoughts real?

We try to make sense of the world around us; we interpret the messages we receive and use these to decide on the best ways of coping with our environment. Sometimes what we think is not really what is happening. There is often more than one way to look at a situation. The way we see the world shapes what we do. Once we realize this we have more choices about the way we behave and can make better decisions.

Look at Figure 4. Is it the face of a woman or a man blowing a horn?

Perhaps you can only see one image. This exercise is rather like life. Often, we don't see what is right in front of

29

Figure 4.   A woman's face – or a man playing a horn?

our eyes and, even when it is pointed out, it can be hard to change our viewpoint. Time, patience and a little effort can work wonders.

How do my beliefs affect me?

Since the 1950s, psychologists have identified a number of beliefs that people apply to their everyday living. In the trauma field, the three 'life beliefs', which have been identified as being crucial to the speed at which a person can recover from a traumatic incident, are:

- bad things happen to 'other people';
- life has meaning and purpose;
- I would always 'do the right thing' in an emergency.

All of these beliefs cause their own particular type of problems. For example, bad things *don't* just happen to 'other people' – they can happen to *anyone*. Someone has to be a statistic and *bad things happen to good people and good people sometimes do bad things.*

If we believe that 'life has meaning and purpose', then person-made disasters and acts of cruelty or senseless bloodshed can be greatly disturbing. Such incidents seem meaningless and with no purpose.

For those who believe they would 'do the right thing' in an emergency this belief can become challenged when they find themselves behaving in a different way to the way they would have predicted.

As mentioned earlier, some of these involuntary and uncontrollable reactions are pre-programmed by our biology. When we are in a life-threatening situation, our stress response kicks in and our body becomes like an alarm system. Either we flee to escape danger or we stay and stand our ground. Either way, it is almost impossible for anyone to predict with any accuracy how he/she will behave in a life-threatening situation.

Human beings tend to use beliefs to guide everyday transactions. For example, '*I will go to work and come home safe*' or '*I will drive to work quite safely*'. We may find our thinking becomes distorted if our beliefs are challenged by life events that, in turn, can cause us to become hyper-aroused and hyperactive. Anxiety can be a common feature of such thinking.

As mentioned earlier, beliefs are formed from the messages we receive as children from those around us. It is these messages that shape the way we think about ourselves.

Faulty thinking

Two people are late for an appointment due to an unexpected traffic holdup. One might recognize that there is nothing that can be done, uses his hands-free mobile to phone the people he needs to inform about the delay, and then switches on the radio to listen to his favourite radio station. The other gets nervous, starts to tell himself that this is awful and that others will think badly of him. He becomes so upset he does not think about using his mobile. Both men experience the same situation but the way they think about it either helps them or hinders.

Faulty thinking relates to the way in which we interpret situations, and the following considers the ways in which we can change our thinking to that which is likely to be more effective in dealing with anxiety.

Healthy thinking

Simple as ABC

There is a model used in Cognitive–Behavioural Therapy called the ABC model. The following describes how situations trigger thoughts, how thoughts trigger feelings and how feelings lead to actions.

A	B	C
Situation	Thoughts based on beliefs	Consequences
(*e.g. looking at an invitation to a party*)	(*e.g. I won't have anything to say and people will think there is something wrong with me*	feelings (*e.g. anxiety*) actions (*e.g. deciding not to go*)

Negative thoughts

Much of our thinking is in the form of automatic thoughts. We use the term automatic as we are often not conscious of such thinking. These thoughts simply seem to 'pop' into our head. In a way it is rather like shop music – something in the background of which we are not really aware.

Negative automatic thoughts are often referred to as NATs. In many ways this is a good description for such thoughts as, rather like the insects, they are irritating. Although you do not often see them, their bites can irritate for days. These kinds of thoughts are usually distorted – that is to say they do not match the facts. They are involuntary and therefore it can be difficult to switch them off.

As we have had many years to perfect our thinking styles it can be hard to change the way we think. If you have ever tried to break a habit you will appreciate how hard it can be.

Types of negative thinking

There are many types of negative thoughts. You may find you relate to some more than others.

All or nothing thinking

You see things in extreme terms such as good or bad, right or wrong, success or failure. You probably set impossible tasks and then feel bad when you do not achieve them. You may even not start tasks because you feel you cannot complete them to the desired standard.

33

For example:

- You planned how to deal with a social event and although you have done really well you misunderstand what someone says to you and feel stupid – you say to yourself '*Well that's it – I've blown it*'.
- You may be struggling with a diet and find that you have eaten two biscuits. You then say to yourself, '*I might as well finish them all now that I've broken my diet, I'm so useless*'.

EXERCISE

If you decide that *all or nothing* thinking relates to you, in your notebook list two situations where you can identify this type of thinking, together with the thoughts that were going through your head at the time.

Jumping to conclusions

This is rather like believing you are telepathic and can read minds. You predict a negative outcome and then encourage it to happen by telling yourself it will. In effect, you set up what could be called a 'self-fulfilling prophecy'.

For example:

- You have to make a comment about a project at work and find yourself thinking about everything that could go wrong. As you do this you feel more and more anxious and then discover that all the things you have told yourself will happen come true!
- You are out on a date for the first time and the person you are with seems a little withdrawn. You think '*He's*

disappointed with me, as he thinks I am not very interesting.' In fact, however, he has had some bad news and does not realize it has upset him as much as it has. Because you believe it is you, the situation deteriorates between you.

EXERCISE

If you decide that *jumping to conclusions* relates to you, list two situations where you can identify this type of thinking, together with the thoughts that were going through your mind at the time.

Mental filter

A mental filter is like a sieve where you filter out everything that's good and focus only on the negative things that have happened.

For example:

- Your friend tells you how much she appreciates you and all the things she likes about you and then mentions in passing that she wishes you would stand up for yourself. You find yourself obsessing about the one comment she made that you feel is negative while ignoring the rest.
- You want to learn another language but remember that you had problems at school. Although there are many other examples of how quickly you learn, on the basis of this experience you predict that you will be useless and do not join the class.

EXERCISE

If you decide that *mental filter* relates to you, list two situations where you can identify this type of thinking, together with the thoughts that were going through your mind at the time.

Discounting the positive

You make yourself feel unhappy by discounting your achievements and the positive things you have done. When we discount the positive we take the pleasure out of life.

For example:

- You have been working hard to overcome your anxiety and you manage to go to a family party and deal with the people there. However, you say to yourself *'that was nothing, anyone could have done that'.*
- You have had a busy day at the office. Although you have managed to get on top of many of the items on your list it was impossible to clear them all. You tell yourself *'I've achieved nothing today.'*

EXERCISE

If you decide that *discounting the positive* relates to you, list two situations where you can identify this type of thinking together with the thoughts that were going through your mind at the time.

Emotional reasoning

You believe that what you feel is true. So if you feel bad you believe it's because you have done something wrong.

For example:

- You feel anxious about meeting new people and therefore conclude you are inferior to other people.
- You make a mistake and you find yourself thinking '*I made a mistake, therefore I am a failure.*'

EXERCISE

If you decide that *emotional reasoning* relates to you, list two situations where you can identify this type of thinking, together with the thoughts that were going through your mind at the time.

Labelling

Do you label yourself with terms such as '*I am a failure*'; '*I am useless*'; and '*I am worthless*'? Every time anything goes wrong, however small, it reinforces the label you have given yourself.

For example:

- You did not do as well as you could have done at school and feel a failure. Because you did not do well, you say to yourself '*I am a failure*'.
- You made a mistake and because of this you say to yourself '*I am stupid*'.

EXERCISE

If you decide that *labelling* relates to you, list two situations where you can identify this type of thinking, together with the thoughts that were going through your mind at the time.

Personalization and blame

You take everything personally and blame yourself even when it isn't your fault.

For example:

● You are in charge of organizing a holiday and have had a number of setbacks caused by your friends' inability to decide on aspects of the trip. A few of your friends are a little agitated and you find yourself feeling anxious, thinking, '*I am pretty useless. I should have managed to organize things better and my friends think I am stupid*'.

EXERCISE

If you decide that personalization and blame relate to you, list two situations where you can identify this type of thinking together with the thoughts that were going through your mind at the time.

Over-generalization

You tend to be prone to making global statements about yourself, other people and the world.

For example:

- You are struggling with a new accounting system. You make a mistake and think, '*I always get things wrong!*'
- Your last relationship ended because you found out your girlfriend was cheating and you think, '*women aren't trustworthy*'.

EXERCISE

If you decide that over-generalizing relates to you, list two situations where you can identify this type of thinking together with the thoughts that were going through your mind at the time.

Shoulds and musts

Your life is full of things you think you '*should*' *be* and '*must*' *do*. You use these statements as a way of trying to motivate yourself. However, the more you tell yourself these things the less likely you are to do them. In addition, you also end up feeling bad about yourself. Some people use 'shoulds' and 'musts' as a way of thinking about other people in a punishing way. For example, *he should have known, she must do what I want*. When we use this type of thinking in relation to others we are really saying we know what is right.

For example:

- You spend time believing '*I should not feel anxious about this type of thing at my age. I have to take care of others*'.

● You are having a particularly difficult time and you start thinking '*I must get a grip. I should be able to deal with all this*'.

EXERCISE

If you decide that *shoulds and musts* relate to you, list two situations where you can identify this type of thinking, together with the thoughts that were going through your mind at the time.

Catastrophizing

When we use this type of thinking it is rather like making a mountain out of a molehill – if there is a way of making things as bad as possible we think it. People using this type of thinking often use lots of emotional words that predict the most awful consequences.

For example:

● Your boss says he wants to talk to you tomorrow and you spend the evening worrying about what you have done, imagining all kinds of awful things.
● You promise to collect some non-essential dry cleaning for a friend but forget, and you behave as if it is the end of the world and not simply a minor setback.

EXERCISE

If you decide that *catastrophizing* relates to you, list two situations where you can identify this type of thinking, together with the thoughts that were going through your mind at the time.

Anxiety-free thinking means learning how to challenge and change your negative thinking. Try to imagine that every time you engage in negative thinking it's like going to your building society, taking out a handful of hard-earned cash and then giving it away without thought. Your emotional energy is just as valuable. It's when you face a crisis that you need to be able to call upon your reserves. After all, it's when the central heating needs replacing that you are glad you have saved some money, and the same principle applies when you face an emotional crisis.

Edit your thoughts

Writing things down means you are more likely to stick to your plans. Buy yourself a notebook and use this to track your progress. If you keep all your information in one place it means that when you have a bad day, where you feel you are slipping back and making no progress, you have an independent record of your success. Everyone has bad days and progress hardly ever goes in a straight line upwards. There are usually some setbacks along the way.

Your first step is to learn *how to* challenge your thoughts. Using the list you made of your negative think-ing under the 'self-defeating thinking' list, copy into your notebook and complete the 'Faulty thinking form' below to help you identify the type of unhelpful thinking in which you are engaging.

Faulty thinking form

Situation	Self defeating thinking	Feelings and actions	Healthy response	New approach
A	B	C	D	E

Completed example

Situation A	Self defeating thinking B	Feelings and actions C	Healthy response D	New approach E
Being asked to a party	*I won't know anyone. I'm really not good at meeting people, I will have nothing to say and they will think I am boring.* **CHALLENGES** **Empirical:** *Where's my evidence that people will think I am boring?* **Logical:** *Just because I don't like parties how does it logically follow that I'm not good at meeting people?* **Pragmatic:** *Does holding on to these ideas make my life better or worse?*	**Anxiety** *Even if I*	**Empirical:** *There is no evidence that people will think I am boring. If I ask people about them- selves it will show them I am interested in them.* **Logical:** *I meet new people at work and manage OK, so if I use the same skills it is logical that I will handle things OK* **Pragmatic** powerful. I *find it hard it is not the end of the world.*	If I plan for the party then I can handle it. If I use the skills I have learnt at work and ask people about themselves then they will think I am inter- ested in them. If I do not go to the party I am only allowing my fear to become more will never learn to feel better about such events if I do not practise dealing with them.

Challenge your thoughts

Jumping to conclusions

Look for EVIDENCE to challenge your thinking. If you believe you *'always get things wrong'*, think about occasions when you *'got things right'*. Check out your thinking by asking people what they really think rather than simply acting on what you believe – your beliefs are only assumptions.

Overgeneralization

Learn to be your own best friend. Ask yourself what you would say to a friend in the same position. Don't you think it is strange that we are often kinder to others than we are to ourselves?

Shoulds and musts

Use the idea of 'preference' versus 'absolutist' statements like 'should'. When you use 'should' you are really saying that the world and the people in it (including yourself) absolutely must behave a certain way. For example, *'I really would prefer to get things right all the time'* instead of *'I must not get things wrong'*. There is nothing wrong with wanting to do well or wanting others to do the things we would want them to do. However, there is no rule that other people should do what we want, or that just because we want something we should have it!

All or nothing

When you find yourself thinking in an extreme way, look for the middle route. For example, could you break the

43

task down into stages? Did you manage to do some of what you set out to do? If so, give yourself credit for what you *have* done.

Mental filter

Challenge your filter by writing down three good things that have happened each day. Watch out and listen for positive comments and when you find yourself worrying about something someone has said, ask yourself if you are ignoring the positive comments.

Discounting the positive

When you tell yourself that what you have done doesn't count, stop and give yourself a pat on the back. Make a point of finding someone to speak to out loud about what you have done. For example, '*I am really pleased with the way I spoke up*'.

Emotional reasoning/labelling

When you call yourself a negative name like stupid, a failure, or no-good, ask yourself what you *really* mean. After all, what makes someone a failure? You can fail at something like an exam but failing *at* something is not a failure. It does not discount the positive.

The 'Big I, little I' exercise (Figure 5) can be useful. Draw the outline of a large 'I' – this Big 'I' represents you – then fill the 'I' in with lots of little 'i's, which represent different parts of your personality. For example, 'I am kind', 'I can cook', 'I have a good sense of humour'.

Personalization and blame

When you find yourself blaming yourself (or other people) because you believe it is your entire fault, draw a

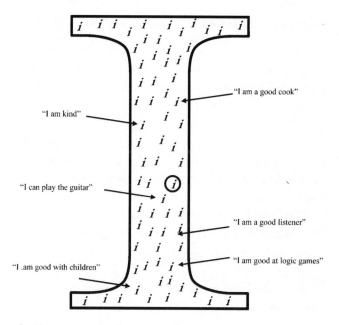

Figure 5.   Big I little i diagram

'responsibility pie'. Think about all the factors of the situation and how many people or circumstances have contributed to the outcome. As you carve up the pie you will see that you are only one part of a much bigger system. Only take responsibility for what is yours, learn from the situation for next time, and speak to others about their part.

When you have worked out what actions belong to whom, take responsibility for what is yours and give back the responsibility that belongs to other people. Allocate a percentage to each of the people and/or areas you have identified.

Below are some useful questions to ask yourself.

What's the situation?

'I feel anxious and responsible because my boss was upset with me or for not arriving on time to a meeting with a client. I explained that I had been held up in traffic but he still feels I let him down.'

What did you try to do?

I tried to ring on my mobile but only got his voicemail. I tried ringing a colleague but she did not answer her mobile. I did get through to the company we were visiting and left a message at reception.

What part do you think you played in the situation?

I could have left a little more time to get to the venue.

Me = thirty per cent

What part do other people or circumstances play?

My boss did change the time and I had to alter a number of my appointments to fit in. He did not check with me personally but left a message on my voicemail and did not check to see if the change of time was convenient to me.

Boss = thirty per cent

There was an unexpected problem with an overturned lorry, which slowed the traffic down.

Roadworks = forty per cent

Catastrophizing

Notice the emotive language you are using and tone it down. Remember that things are not awful, a disaster, or a nightmare. This does not mean that the situation is not difficult, hard, or painful. Use words that put the situation

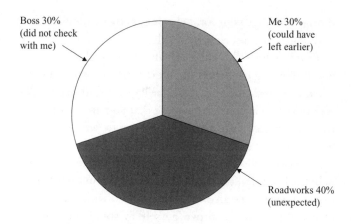

Boss 30%
(did not check
with me)

Me 30%
(could have
left earlier)

Roadworks 40%
(unexpected)

Figure 6.   Ressponsibility pie chart

into perspective. Ask yourself '*What's the worst that can really happen?*'

Life rules

Some people hold negative beliefs about themselves. For example, you may believe you are a failure, worthless, a bad person, stupid, unlovable, or unattractive. These beliefs shape your actions in everyday life. They can be seen as the rules that dictate the way we manage our daily lives.

An example of a life rule would be if you thought you were a failure and then spent your life avoiding situations for fear of being found out. You may live your life believing that '*I must avoid being found out*', and that criticism from other people means you are in danger of being found out. '*My friends keep telling me to go for a promotion but if I do they will find out I am useless and will realize I am a failure.*' You may give up on life, be miserable, and avoid trying to change your lot, believing that you are incapable of doing so because you are a failure.

People whose life rules are about over-achieving as a way of fending off beliefs of failure tend to feel good only when they *are* achieving. If you believe yourself to be lacking in some way you may believe that you are a worthless person because you do not conform to whatever you believe the standard to be.

A person who believes that she is only safe from her beliefs about failure if she avoids situations may find herself feeling very anxious if she is faced with a situation where she needs to prove herself in some way. Some people believe they are bad people and that if people really knew them, rather than the mask they present to the world, they would be disliked and seen as a fraud. It is helpful to identify your basic beliefs so that you can use the countermeasures described in this book to change the ways you perceive yourself.

Beliefs about yourself, others and the world have been formed by the messages you received from:

- family
- friends
- the world.

Over time you have been conditioned to think in a certain way and it takes time to change your belief, regardless of how motivated you are to do so.

Demands that may increase your anxiety

There are three types of demands we make of ourselves in the form of 'musts' These are:

Demands about self – e.g., '*I must always get it right*' (creates stress, anxiety, shame and guilt).

Demands about others – e.g., '*You must behave well otherwise it's awful*' (creates anger).

Demands about the world – e.g., '*The world should be a fair and just place*' (creates self pity, addictive behaviour and depression).

To help you identify your personal musts and the types of beliefs your musts are based on, write yourself an '*I must otherwise I am*' list as follows.

Demands of self

I must .... otherwise ....
e.g., *I must be strong and capable, otherwise I am a failure.*

Demands of others

You must .... otherwise ....
e.g., *You must agree with me, otherwise I am wrong and that would be awful.*

Demands of the world

The world must .... otherwise ....
e.g., *The world must treat me well if I work hard and do my best otherwise it's not fair.*

When you have identified the personal demands you make of yourself, others and the world, you need to set about challenging them. Do this in the same way you identified your automatic negative thoughts earlier.

Challenging your demands

You can challenge the demands you are making of yourself in the following ways:

- Consider the impact your demand has on you and those around you.
- Identify how you know when the demand is activated (i.e., the thoughts, feelings and behaviours you experience).
- Think about how the demand came about and the life experiences that sustain it.
- Consider the advantages and disadvantages of holding on to your demand.
- Identify a more appropriate way of rephrasing your demand, which fits with life as it is now.
- Think about how you are going to put your new demand into action.

What if I can't identify a demand but suspect there is one?

Sometimes you find yourself saying things like: '*It would be awful*' or '*That's just not right*'. When you make statements like these it doesn't seem at first sight as if there is a core belief in operation. You could find that a situation triggers a strong feeling and, although you identify your negative automatic thought and challenge it, you still seem to feel unhappy.

If this is the case, ask yourself a series of questions and, rather like an archaeological dig, these will help you uncover your core belief. It is sometimes helpful to see your thought at the beginning of a long chain and your core beliefs at the other end. You have to identify each link in the chain and, as you do so, you get nearer the end of the chain that holds your core belief.

For example:

Situation: You are offered a transfer to a new branch at work that could lead to a permanent promotion, but you quickly refuse.

Feeling: Anxiety.

Thought: I could never do that – I wouldn't be able to cope.

1	Ask yourself:	*'What would be scary about taking the job?'*
	Answer:	*'I would not be able to do it.'*
2	Ask yourself:	*'Supposing that were true, what would that mean?'*
	Answer:	*'People would think me stupid.'*
3	Ask yourself:	*'And if they did think you were stupid, what would that mean?'*
	Answer:	*'People would laugh at me.'*
4	Ask yourself:	*'And if they did?'*
	Answer:	*'That would be awful.'*
5	Ask yourself:	*'What would be awful?'*
	Answer:	*'They would think I was not capable.'*
6	Ask yourself:	*'Suppose they did think you weren't capable?'*
	Answer:	*'They would know how dumb I am so I would rather not put myself in that position.'*
7	Ask yourself:	*'So what does it mean to me not to put myself in that position?'*
	Answer:	*'I must not take risks otherwise people will know I am a failure.'*

You end up with a core belief that, in this case, is 'I must not take risks and be laughed at, otherwise people will know I am a failure'.

Summary

One way of looking at the role self-defeating thinking plays in shaping your life is to consider the relationship between automatic thoughts, demands/life rules and core beliefs. Core beliefs are the conclusions you draw about yourself as a person, as in thinking you are basically bad, worthless or a failure.

Automatic thoughts are triggered by the situations you find yourself in; for example, being asked to do something you do not want to do but thinking 'I should do what my friend wants'. Another way of thinking about demands is to see them as 'if/then' rules; for example, '*If I always get things right then people will think well of me*'. Core beliefs are absolutist beliefs that we hold about ourselves such as '*I did not get that promotion, which means I am a failure*'.

A simple way of thinking of this three-stage model is outlined in Figure 7.

Learn to accept yourself

The tips on the pages that follow are based on the principles of a therapy called Rational Emotive Behaviour Therapy, or REBT for short. They offer practical suggestions and ways to begin the process of self-acceptance. You need to learn to like yourself and to do this you need to accept yourself. Self-acceptance is the arduous process of learning to like yourself 'warts and all'. Self-acceptance helps you to decrease your anxiety and increase your confidence.

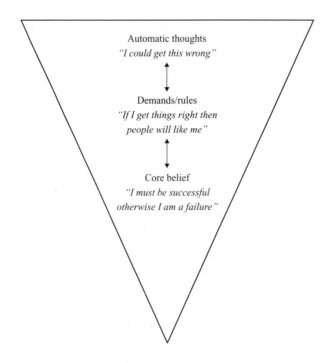

Automatic thoughts
"I could get this wrong"

Demands/rules
*"If I get things right then
people will like me"*

Core belief
*"I must be successful
otherwise I am a failure"*

Figure 7.   Three-stage model of core beliefs

Tips to help you like yourself

● Remember that human beings are not perfect and that
includes you! There is no such thing as a person who is
100% right, good, capable or strong. If you spend your
life believing that perfection exists you will always be
disappointed, unhappy, stressed and in danger of being
anxious and depressed. There is nothing wrong with
wanting to do things well or be a good worker, student,
parent, partner or friend. Set yourself realistically high
but not impossibly perfectionist standards.

- Remember that everyone is equal, regardless of ability. It is possible for someone to have greater talents or skills than you without being a *better person*. Stop comparing yourself to other people as this can only lead to feelings of anxiety, resentment or disappointment. If you admire someone for something they have done there is nothing wrong with thinking about the quality they possess or the way they did something, trying to identify the key components so that you can model your behaviour on theirs and learn from what they have done. Modelling yourself is not the same as comparing yourself. There may be differences in what people can do but there is no difference in the basic worth of each human being. One person is not 'better' than another.

- There is no such thing as a 'global rating' on human goodness or badness. No one is ever *all good* or *all bad*. Good people sometimes do bad things and bad people sometimes do good things. If you behave in a way that you think better about then take the appropriate action. For example: apologize, explain and see what you can do to put things right. However, doing something you later regret does not make you a bad person, just as doing one good deed does not make someone a saint. If you keep on seeing yourself and/or others in this all or nothing way, you place unrealistic pressure on yourself and on others.

- Over-generalization (see pages 40–41) is where you exaggerate one aspect of your behaviour (e.g., *Because I felt scared. I am a weak person*). If you want to conquer your anxiety, it is important that you do not judge the *whole* of you on just one *part* of your behaviour; for example, *I was scared but even though I was scared I did what needed doing.* Keep things in proportion. Blowing things out of proportion wastes time and energy. Confident people deal with situations.

- Remember to work on dropping the *shoulds* and *musts,* as all they do is lead you to develop a conditional outlook on yourself. Dropping *shoulds*, *musts* and *have tos* does not mean abdicating your responsibilities – it simply means stopping putting yourself down.
- Remember that self-acceptance is hard work. It requires energy and commitment and consistent work to make it happen.

You also need to:

- Learn to respect yourself – you are as valuable as everyone else
- Live a lifestyle that is supportive of your health – there is no point making yourself ill from overwork or abusing your body. If you do this you are likely to increase your anxiety. For example, caffeine products are likely to increase your susceptibility to anxiety. Caffeine is a stimulant and, as people who are anxious produce adrenaline (as we saw earlier when considering the stress response), such stimulants help to increase the production of adrenaline.
- Engage in supportive relationships and carry out the life audit that follows. Work at your relationships, make sure you have a variety and cultivate them as you would your garden plants. Tending to friendships pays you back ten-fold with the love and concern others will feel and show towards you.
- Set goals for yourself that are specifically designed to improve your life and diminish your anxiety. When

you undertake your annual life audit, set yourself a series of goals for the year. Decide what you want to change and how you will do it. The changes that you make and what you learn about yourself all go towards your developing new life skills and increasing your confidence.

- Recognize that change cannot be achieved overnight and that you will need to keep on working at challenging negative attitudes about yourself. I know this has been said more than once, but that's because it is so important.

- Spend time and money on yourself – you are worth it! Learn to pamper yourself. You probably spoil other people, so why not yourself?

- Remember that you need to take responsibility for your own life. It is all too easy to blame other people or 'bad luck' for situations. However bad your situation, you *do* have choices. Sometimes it is just too easy to stay in a 'victim role'. Sometimes you have to give yourself what I call a 'therapeutic kick up the backside' When things go wrong it is helpful to allow yourself to feel your feelings, to express your emotions appropriately, and to seek support from others. It is not helpful to spend time feeling sorry for yourself. There is a major difference between self-pity and self-concern.

Ask yourself if there is a payoff for continuing to engage in a particular behaviour. For example, if you allow others to make all the decisions for you, the payoff may be that you never have to face 'being in the wrong', and you can always blame them for the way things have turned out.

Learn to appreciate yourself

If you have been lacking in confidence for a long time you may find it hard to identify and appreciate your good points. Go back to page 44 and complete the 'Big I, Little I' exercise if you have not done so already. If you need more help ask yourself the following questions.

- *What am I able to do?*
- *What do I like about myself?*
- *What have I learnt in life?*
- *How would someone else describe me?*
- *How will I ensure I actually practise these skills – what might get in the way?*

The life audit

The 'life audit' is a technique to help you identify the areas of your life you would benefit from changing. A life audit should be undertaken on an annual basis, with quarterly 'check-ups' to monitor progress.

A life audit is a way of working out what in life you are happy with, need to get more of or need to stop doing. Once you have completed the audit itself, the next step is to set about making changes to those areas of your life you have identified as needing attention. There is no point working out what you like or dislike unless you are prepared to change the things you are unhappy about and increase the things you like. People who suffer from anxiety very often just let life happen, feeling they have no control over what they do. The life audit is one way for you to take up that control.

EXERCISE

Write down all the things you like and dislike about each of the following eight areas of your life:

- Living environment (*e.g., flat, house, geographical area*)
- Family (*e.g,. family of origin, children*)
- Personal relationship(s) (*e.g., partner*)
- Friends/social life (*e.g., friendships, hobbies, outings*)
- Work/career (*e.g., current job, future aspirations*)
- Finances (*e.g., budgeting, savings, pensions, investments*)
- Health (*e.g., diet, exercise, stress management*)
- Inner soul/spirit (*e.g., your sense of purpose in life*)

Example – Life Audit

Work/career

Like	Dislike
My colleagues	Having done the same repetitive tasks for some time
Close to home	Not speaking up at weekly meetings
Spacious environment	

Consider each of the things you don't like and ask yourself what you could do to change the situation. Research suggests that you are far more likely to carry out your plans if you write them down.

Action plans

Work/career

Dislike	Action plan
Not speaking up at meetings	Need to think about this before I go to the meeting so that I have my comments worked out ahead of time.

Distraction

Distraction techniques are helpful when you are worried and keep having thoughts that are making you feel uncomfortable or are undermining your efforts. Distraction is a way if taking your attention away from what is happening on to something else. If you take your attention away from your symptoms they often diminish. When you find yourself in this position, you need to decide not to think about your thoughts and then engage your mind with something else. Have you ever been in a situation where you have felt better because you were doing something else?

There are three types of distraction:

1. Paying attention to what is going on around you – try guessing the ages of people in the room, or listen to someone else's conversation, or decide to count as many round objects as you can see in the room.
2. Physical activity – try cleaning, tidying up, or finding tasks to do.
3. Engage in some form or mental activity – recite your times tables, say the alphabet backwards or do a crossword.

ANXIETY-FREE EMOTIONS

Learn to be emotionally smart

Emotional Intelligence is about learning to being emotionally smart. It is not always the person with the highest IQ who does best. Emotionally smart people get the most from managing their own and other people's emotions. If you can learn the skills of emotional smartness it will help you overcome your anxiety.

The skills fall into five key areas, examined below.

Identifying your emotions

Emotionally smart people are able to identify their own emotions. This means learning to tell other people how you feel. It means taking responsibility for your own emotions by starting sentences with '*I feel . . .*'

Exercise

How to identify emotions

1. Look at the series of positive and negative words below. Make a note of the words you think describe you best.
2. Why have you chosen those particular words?
3. If you were to change your negative words to positive ones what would you have to do?

Positive	Negative
Empathic	Angry
Loving	Anxious
Happy	Jealous

Positive	Negative
Joyful	Possessive
Caring	Remorseful
Enthusiastic	Envious
Warm	Resentful

Managing your emotions

Emotions can be difficult and emotionally smart people know when to take care of themselves. For example, when you have had a difficult day what are the things you do to take care of yourself? Do you have a long hot bath and relax? Do you talk to a friend? Do you get a DVD or video and watch that? There are times when you need to take care of other people's emotions and there are times when you need to motivate yourself and others.

Exercise

Taking care of my emotions

List two ways in which you take care of yourself and two ways in which you take care of other people (e.g., warm bath, ring a friend, encourage someone to talk).

Managing other people's emotions

People who are anxious often spend so much time worrying about what is happening to them that they can miss the benefits of taking in the environment around them. Emotionally smart people have developed the ability to

61

pick up other people's emotions. Using skills such as empathy (the ability to imagine what it might feel like to see the world from another perspective), a smart person considers how the other person might be feeling, realizing that such recognition can encourage a more co-operative relationship. It is true that some anxious people are very good at being sensitive to others but have lost contact with the importance of their own needs.

Exercise

How do I show my understanding of others?

Think about people and situations where you feel a connection with what the person is feeling. This ability of being able to imagine what it is like for the other person is called empathy. Choose friends or use characters from films or television, then list their names. Think about why you empathize with the people you have chosen, and write these reasons against each person's name.

Now, list all the ways in which you would demonstrate your understanding to another person (e.g., *giving the person my full attention or using certain words*).

Learning to motivate yourself

There are times when strong emotions get in the way. There may be times when it is better to put off your own needs and wants for a future pay-off. Some people find themselves so caught up in their immediate emotions that they forget there is a bigger picture. Anxious people often do this but for the wrong reasons – more because of their own fears rather than as a life strategy.

Exercise

When have I motivated myself or others?

Think of two situations where you have motivated yourself or other people. In particular, think of situations where there have been strong emotions. How did you cope with the strong emotion so that you were able to complete the task in hand? Structure your notes in the following way.

Situation 1
What happened.
What I did.

Situation 2
What happened.
What I did.

Healthy relationships

Life is full of relationships so it makes sense to consider the behaviours that help create happy and productive relationships while recognising those that destroy them.

Exercise

Ways of creating positive relationships

List three ways to cultivate a relationship (e.g., ringing people regularly, remembering special events, or listening to a friend's problems)

Learning to appreciate yourself and others

How do you feel when I ask you to:

(a) list five things you could do better;

(b) list five things that have gone well and you are pleased with?

I suspect you found the first question easier to answer and the second more difficult. Most people neglect the power of praise and appreciation – the bottom line is that appreciation and praise motivate.

Some people fear that if they praise themselves or others it will lead to a slacking off in effort. It is well documented that children who are constantly criticized are more likely to have poor confidence and to stop trying to improve. They may even feel anxious about getting things wrong.

Success encourages success and every time you or someone else does something well (even partially well) it is one more step towards building an anxiety-free life.

Exercise

Past praise

Write in your notebook, completing each sentence appropriately:

1. The last time I praised myself was . . .
2. The last time I praised someone else was . . .

Future praise

Think of two things that you know you could praise yourself for and complete the following sentences.
I was pleased with myself when I . . .
I thought I did well to . . .

Exercise

My epitaph

Now write your own epitaph in your notebook. How would you like to be remembered? I've written mine so that you can see what one could look like.

She lived her life with enthusiasm. She cared for others but knew how to have a good time. She had a go even when she was scared and she is remembered with love.

When you wrote your epitaph what feelings came up for you? Look at what you have written and consider whether you are living your life in a way that is likely to make your words come true. What changes do you need to make and how will you set about making those changes?

Other people's emotions

If you have the ability to read and understand other people's emotions you have a great advantage in influencing people's attitudes towards you.

Reading emotions means:

1. *Watching body language*
People's body language and voice tone tell you a lot about how they are feeling and your body language is also a way of communicating. Anxious people often hide away from others – they avert their gaze and look to the floor or they try to make themselves as small as they can in the hope they will not be noticed.

2. *Listening to the words*

What do the words tell you? Sometimes people tell you what they are feeling (e.g., '*I feel scared about trying that*'). If you think of the words you use what impact do you think they have? What do they say about you?

3. *Using your empathy*

Empathy, as we explored earlier, is the ability to imagine what it might be like to see the world wearing someone else's shoes. Empathy can be expressed through statements such as '*You sound sad about that*' and '*I imagine you were really scared*'.

How to deal with strong emotion

Strong emotions can be disturbing for both the person experiencing them and for those around at the time. Many people feel uncomfortable with expressing emotions or being around people who are expressing them.

Strong emotions could include anxiety, anger, or severe emotional distress. Sometimes you may be frightened by the strength of the emotion you feel; for example, being overwhelmed with fear. Being around an anxious person can be difficult, as anxiety can often be felt by others and this can either make the other person feel anxious or make them cut the contact short as they find it an uncomfortable emotion.

It is easier to handle strong emotions if you make a point of acknowledging them. If you suppress feelings, never admitting them to yourself or others, they get stored. Sooner or later there is simply too much stored emotion and the natural suppression mechanism stops working and a sudden outpouring takes place.

Some people believe they should let all their emotions show all the time. These people lack emotional intelligence as they influence other people's attitudes towards them by being overly dramatic and emotional.

There are, of course, times when strong emotions are understandable; for example, if you had just had bad news or if you needed to defend yourself against violent attack.

Exercise

When was the last time you felt a strong emotion?

Think of the last time you experienced a strong emotion – what had happened? What did you feel? How did you deal with your emotion and what was the outcome? When you have completed the exercise, look at your reactions and ask yourself whether you are happy with what you did. If you are not happy what you could have done differently? Structure your notes in the following way.

What actually happened.
What I felt at the time.
What I did at the time.
Outcome.
What could I have done differently?

Don't put things off!!!

Anxiety is overcome by tackling life as much as you can head on. Make a list of all the things you have put off. Procrastination tends to compound problems. The more you mean to do but never get around to doing the more your anxiety is likely to grow. If you have a lot of things on your list you cannot do them all at once, so why not rate them in terms of difficulty, for example by using a scale of 0–10:

0 1 2 3 4 5 6 7 8 9 10

(0 = easy and 10 = really hard)

Examples:
Joining an evening class   = 3
Completing a report   = 5
Booking a holiday on your own   = 7

Once you have drawn up this list, start with items that have a rating of between three and seven. Anything rated more than a seven may be too difficult for you at the beginning of the process. Conversely, anything less than a three may be too easy.

Always remember to praise yourself on your achievements. Think about *what you have* managed to do rather than what you believe you *should* have been doing. Keeping this kind of a record provides you with evidence of the goals you have set and your success in dealing with them.

Everyone has bad days, days when you feel that nothing has been achieved or changed. By keeping these details in your journal you have a written record of the improvements you have made and these help you evaluate your progress realistically.

Get moving

Apart from exercise being physically healthy it is also good for our psychological well-being. Research suggests that even mild exercise can have a positive effect. Simply walking a couple of miles each day and walking up and down stairs can do the trick. Exercise not only relieves stress, it also releases naturally produced chemicals that can raise your moods and help reduce adrenaline levels that have been heightened because of anxiety.

Guilt

Some people who are anxious also feel guilty. We often say that we feel guilty but guilt is not so much a feeling as a thought process. When you say you feel guilty it usually means:

- You have broken one of your value rules, e.g., *'I must always be kind and think of other people's feelings ahead of my own'*.
- You think only about the outcome of what you believe you have done or not done, e.g., *'I should have known he would be unhappy'*.

These types of guilt are either about the *actions you have taken* or the *choices you have made* and the consequences of your choices. A value rule is part of the moral code by which you live your life, whereas an outcome is more about what you have done.

There are some people who believe they are guilty simply because they are alive. Someone who feels guilty but cannot tell you why may be experiencing this kind of guilt. This type of guilt stays with such people throughout life unless they change the way they think about themselves and the world.

If you've made a mistake, it makes sense to put it right. Try and do something to put the situation right. If you simply feel guilty without taking action you are likely to avoid people, places, and activities that remind you of the guilt you feel.

You can deal with guilt by

- Asking yourself what you actually feel guilty about.
- Asking yourself if you were to find yourself in exactly the same situation today would you behave any differently?
- Thinking about the way your core beliefs influence the way you live your life and whether it is possible for anyone to live up to all of those core beliefs all of the time.
- Remembering '*bad things happen to good people and good people sometimes do bad things*'.
- Examining your 'thinking style' for examples of the kind of self-defeating thoughts described on page 43.
- Remembering you are a fallible human being.
- Realising that if there is something you can do to change the situation for others, then doing so.
- Not hiding away from the world – it won't make things better, just make you feel worse.
- Learning to forgive yourself and remembering that forgiveness is a choice

Use the 'Big I, Little i' on page 44 to remind yourself of your positive points and use the 'Responsibility Pie' on page 46 to help you work out who is responsible for what.

Cost–benefit analysis

It can be hard to change your behaviour, particularly if you have been acting in a certain way for a long time. A 'cost–benefit analysis' can help you identify the costs and the benefits of behaving in a certain way.

Write out your own cost–benefit sheet, using the model shown below, to work out what is happening. You can write down all the benefits of continuing to act the way you are on the right side of the page. Then on the left-hand side of the page you write down all the costs (emotional and practical) of continuing as you are.

Cost–benefit analysis model
Name: Sally Anxious   Date: 8/4/05
Situation: *I don't make decisions in case I am wrong.*

COST	BENEFIT
● Feel anxious	● I can't make a mistake if I don't make a decision
● Other people make the decisions and I don't always like what they decide to do	● I can avoid confrontation
● I feel like a useless person	● People won't be angry with me

Once you have completed both sides of the form you will be in a better position to make decisions about what you want to do. If you want to change you need to decide what you need to do.

The role of assertiveness

Assertiveness means asking for what you want and saying how you feel, while respecting the needs and rights of others. Many people think that being assertive is rather like being in the SAS – you take no prisoners. This is not the case. Anyone who thinks this has aggression mixed up with assertion. Truly assertive people look for what is called a 'win–win' situation and take responsibility for their own actions. Becoming more assertive improves the way we can communicate with others. Most colleges and evening institutes are likely to offer short courses on assertiveness, and there is more about assertion in the next section – 'Anxiety-Free Actions'.

Anxious people are usually passive and are therefore in real need of learning how to become assertive.

Shame and humiliation

You can feel shame because you believe you have broken one of your value rules – one you hold about yourself or one you believe about others. If you believe you have behaved in a way frowned on by friends, family, or society you may feel shame. You may remember the term catastrophizing from the 'Anxiety-Free Thinking' section of this book. You tell yourself that it is 'awful' if you feel a certain thing or have behaved in a certain way. 'Awfulizing' is often expressed in terms of criticism about personal weakness . . . '*If they saw me being so indecisive, that would be awful. What would they think of me?*'

People who experience shame have a great capacity for avoiding people and places that remind them of what they see as their weakness.

Humiliation usually means you believe you have lost status in some way. It is closely linked to the same kind of thought processes connected with shame and guilt, in particular around the issue of worrying about how others will somehow think less of you as a result of your loss of status.

How to deal with shame and humiliation

You can ask yourself:

- Do I really believe someone thinks less of me as a result of what I have done and, if so, why? (Remember to use the skills you have learnt in the 'Anxiety-Free Thinking' section of this book.)
- Would I think less of someone who had gone through an identical experience?

If you have answered 'no' to both questions why hold yourself responsible when you would not treat others the same way?

Dealing with worry

So many people worry about every aspect of life. Anxiety, as we discussed earlier, is based on fear. Things go wrong and there will be times when you are worried. For example, if your partner had to have medical tests it would be normal for you to have some concern regarding outcome. The whole area of fear can be rated in terms of mild, moderate, or severe feelings. Mild fear could be seen as worry, whereas severe fear could be seen as extreme anxiety.

How to worry constructively

Think about the following:

- 39% of the things you worry about never happen;
- 32% of things you worry about have already happened;
- 21% of your worries are over trivialities;
- 9% of your worries relate to important issues where you have legitimate cause for concern.
  (Note: a total of 101% due to rounding up.)

If we stopped worrying this would not be helpful as a certain amount of worry makes you feel better

Your worry notebook

Take any notebook and divide it into four sections using the following headings:

WORRIES FOR TODAY	
1. Things of concern that might happen *The trains might be late. I might not have enough time to complete my report.*	**2. Insignificant things** *I might break one of my nails doing the gardening.*
2. Things that have happened *I had to tell a colleague I could not help due to pressure of work.*	**4. Important things** *Terry and I need to talk about our finances as it looks like my pension plan may not be as solid as I thought.*

Make the entries for headings *one*, *two* and *three* before you go to bed. Choose the time of day you are at your strongest and brightest to complete section *four*.

When it comes to section 4 you need to remember that *worrying about a problem does not solve it – -doing something about it does.* If you do not make a decision to do something positive you can end up making a decision by default. No action still has an outcome. You need to decide whether you want to be in control (as much as is possible), or if you are going to just let things happen. There is *always* a choice.

Relaxation

When you feel anxious it is useful to do some relaxation exercises. There are many forms of relaxation, as we discussed earlier. Some require physical movement while others require nothing more than breathing or visualization techniques. Listed below are three common relaxation techniques.

Often relaxation exercises rely on you being able to make time to lie down or, at least, stop whatever it is that you are doing. This simple breathing exercise is one that you can do anywhere, any time, and no one need know you are doing it. This exercise can help you take the edge off your anxious feelings while reducing the negative effects of adrenaline, helping you maintain your calm. You will remember the breathing exercise in the early section of this book, which provides you with an effective technique to calm you down and help you remain in control. As this exercise is portable, given that you can do it anywhere at any time, it can be termed a 'life saver' as the more you use it the calmer you will feel.

The 'life saver' in action (see also p. 19)

- Breathe in through your nose for a count of four.
- Breathe out through your mouth for a count of five.
- As you breathe out, consciously relax your shoulders.

As you breathe in and out, use your stomach muscles to control your breathing. When breathing in, use your stomach muscles to push out. When you breathe out, use your stomach muscles to push in. This way you breathe more deeply, which helps you gain maximum benefit from the exercise.

People who experience anxiety often breathe shallowly. Shallow breathing means your body gets too much oxygen and many people are tempted to compensate by breathing faster. However, breathing too fast can make you feel dizzy or faint. This leads to a condition called hyperventilation.

Hyperventilation

Hyperventilation means 'over-breathing', something everyone does at some point. For example, when you run to catch a train or do some other kind of physical exertion that requires more oxygen than normal, it's essential to breathe faster. However, when you are feeling anxious you may begin to over-breathe. If too much oxygen enters the bloodstream it upsets the body's mechanism. Too much oxygen means that carbon dioxide levels are depleted and recent research suggests that it is the loss of the carbon dioxide that causes blood vessels to constrict, which, in turn, leads to a sense of dizziness. The 'life saver' breathing exercise helps to prevent you from hyperventilating.

Breathing in a controlled manner is the key to dealing with this unpleasant feeling. Hyperventilation can bring on panic-attack-like symptoms.

This breathing exercise minimizes the effects of hyperventilation. Some people carry a paper bag with them and blow into this when they feel the effects of hyperventilation. Breathing out releases carbon dioxide, so breathing this in again from the bag reduces the levels of oxygen in the blood stream, reducing the effects of the hyperventilation.

It is important to practise your breathing exercises on a daily basis. There is no point in trying out this exercise once and then waiting till you need it before using it again.

Practise your breathing exercises throughout the day, get comfortable with them and you will find how helpful this type of breathing can be in all sorts of situations.

How to use coping imagery to deal with negative emotions

According to research, when you visualize a positive outcome you are more likely to get one. Coping imagery is used as a way of preparing yourself for events. Try the following exercise to see how this works.

Exercise

If you do not have a current or future situation that troubles you, think about the last one that did.

- First, write out a 'fears list' of all the people, places, and situations you feel uncomfortable with or in. Use the 0–10 scale as a way of rating the degree of discomfort you feel (0 = no discomfort and 10 = maximum discomfort).
- Once you have made out your list, choose something that has a rating of no more than 7. (Choosing a higher rating would make it too difficult and choosing a lower rating would not be challenging enough. After all, you want to succeed and if you make your task too difficult you may set yourself up to fail.)
- Now, close your eyes and imagine yourself at the beginning of your task. Use all your senses to imagine the sights, the sounds and the smells. Think about what you would say and what you would do. Think about what you think the other person(s) might say. Use coping strategies like breathing, anchoring and helpful self-talk to help you deal with the event.
- Now practise this visualization two or three times, each time seeing yourself coping with the situation. You may find that practising this exercise actually reduces your original rating even though you are using only your imagination. It is as if your brain is fooled into believing that you really *have done* whatever you set out to do. Once you have practised this exercise a few times the next task is to actually do it!

Maximum benefit is gained from the above technique when you practise it frequently.

If you find it hard to use your imagination, try the following exercise to improve your visualization skills and develop your imagination 'muscles'. Like everything else in life, with practice, your ability will improve.

- Imagine looking at the sky at night
- Choose one star and watch it become brighter and then dimmer. Do this repeatedly.

See if you can track the star across the sky.

ANXIETY-FREE ACTIONS

Graded exposure

If you want to overcome your anxiety you have to challenge your avoidant behaviour. As stated earlier, when we are anxious we want to avoid people, places, and things that trigger our anxiety. The idea of avoidance may seem a sensible one – after all, if you feel bad about doing something it makes sense not to do it. However, when you give in to your feelings all you do is give power to the anxiety and you may well find that as your anxiety increases, your life decreases. For example, you may feel anxious about being in a crowd, so you start avoiding crowds. Next, you find that you don't feel comfortable on the underground so you now travel only by bus. One day, you feel a little anxious on a bus and then stop using the buses and, before you know it, your life is limited. In severe cases this kind of behaviour can lead to conditions such as agoraphobia.

Avoidance can take many forms including not taking up opportunities when they are presented to you, putting things off, not facing up to problems, or not accepting invitations.

If you really want to conquer your anxiety, you need to engage in what is called graded exposure, which means that you start to face those situations you find difficult, engaging in a range of coping strategies to help you deal with your feelings. Research has shown that when you face a feared situation your fear will peak and if you can stay in the situation it will come down after it peaks to a more bearable level. However, when you avoid situations you never get to learn this for yourself.

There are four stages to using graded exposure.

Stage one

Make a list of all the situations you avoid or that make you feel anxious. Then using a scale of 0–8 (0 = no fear and 8 = extreme fear), rate each of the items on the list.

Stage two

Now that you have rated the items place them in order of degree of difficulty.

Stage three

You may want to select the easiest item on your list as the first one to start with. One word of advice here though – it is probably best to start with an item you have rated at four. If you try to deal with anything more than a four it may be too difficult for you to manage. If you start with an item rated at less than four it may be too easy. An item rated four is hard enough for you to get the benefit of the exercise in terms of stretching yourself, but not so high that it is asking too much of you.

Stage four

Plan how you will tackle your task and what coping strategies you will use; for example, breathing, having a coping statement that you will repeat to yourself, or using distraction. Repeat this activity as many times as it takes for you to manage it without difficulty.

When you have succeeded with this item then move on to the next on your list.

The trick with graded exposure is that you must undertake the tasks regularly and for prolonged periods of time so that the anxiety passes.

Sometimes progress may seem slow and you may want to give up. However, progress is progress and giving up will only make matters worse as by doing so you will convince yourself that you cannot cope. One small step at a time is still a step in the right direction. Do not discount what you have achieved. Learning to recognize your achievements, however small you think they are, is a way of increasing your confidence. When you find yourself 'discounting the positives' with statements such as '*Anyone could do this*', say to yourself '*They would find it hard if they experienced the same degree of anxiety as I do*'.

Panic attacks

Panic attacks are extremely common. Differences in the types of symptoms suffered are also extremely common. For example, one person may feel hot, another cold, so general guidelines apply.

Panic attack checklist

If you are experiencing four or more of the of the following symptoms you are probably experiencing panic attacks and would benefit from seeking professional help.

Note: Although panic attacks are distressing, they are not life-threatening. However, as with any unusual physical symptoms, it is always safest to seek the advice of your doctor.

SYMPTOM	YES/NO
Palpitations, fast heart rate	
Sweating	
Shaking	
Shortness of breath	
A choking sensation	
Chest pain	
Nausea	
Feeling dizzy	
Feeling detached and unreal	
Fear of dying	
Tingling sensations	
Chills and/or hot flushes	

Coping with panic attacks

- Remember that a panic attack is no more than an exaggeration of a normal bodily reaction to stress.
- Panic attacks are unpleasant but will not harm you.
- Identify the self-defeating and frightening thoughts you engage in when you experience a panic attack and counter these with the kind of thinking styles set out on pages 41–47 in the section 'Negative thinking'. Adding to your self-defeating thinking will make matters worse, not better.
- Give the fear time to pass. Accept it, knowing that it will go away.
- Don't try and avoid your fear, as this will only make it worse. Facing your fear will help to diminish it, in time.
- When you feel better, plan what to do next.
- Think of the progress you are making every time you face your feelings, then praise yourself for facing your fear.

Gladeana McMahon

Using coping imagery to reduce anxiety

It was mentioned earlier that people who feel anxious often avoid situations. As a result, their lives may become very restricted. Often it requires much more than a simple decision to change that avoidance behaviour.

Confronting a fear head on may prove to be too intimidating. For example, if you are claustrophobic and haven't travelled on public transport for two years, using the rating scale outlined on below (0 = no panic and 8 = major panic), you may experience a rating of seven just thinking about the idea of boarding a tube train.

Trying to force yourself to challenge your fear without making some kind of mental preparation could be enough to tip you over into a full-scale panic attack. A more effective tactic might be to use an imagery technique to prepare you for the event as a way to help decrease your anxiety and practise the type of coping strategies that might be helpful. When anxiety levels have fallen to four or five, using your rating, it might be the time to consider taking a real journey on public transport.

Coping imagery requires a person to imagine him or herself coping in a situation that usually causes them great fear. The following describes the sequence of action for dealing with a specific fear, say fear of travelling on a tube train.

1. First, write out a 'fears list' outlining a hierarchy of feared situations associated with underground travel using a scale of 0–8.

Example: Michelle's list

Thinking about going to the local Underground station=3
Getting my ticket   =4

Standing on the platform	=5
Getting on a tube train	=7
Being stuck in a tunnel	=8

2. Once you have your list made out, choose something that has a rating of no more than four or five. (Choosing anything with a higher rating would make it too difficult. A rating lower than two would probably not be challenging enough.)

Michelle decided to take standing on the platform that she rated as a five. She then went on to imagine the following.

3. Now, close your eyes and imagine yourself standing on the platform. Use all your senses to imagine the people on the platform, the sights and smells. Imagine yourself watching the trains come and go and monitor the anxiety you are feeling. Use coping strategies like breathing, anchoring and helpful self-talk to help yourself stay with the event.

(Michelle had already been taught how to relax through breathing and had anchored a pleasant memory to a ring she always wore. She knew how her body worked, when anxious, in releasing adrenaline into the system and that her physical symptoms were normal. She had also put together some helpful self-talk such as 'This will pass, it is OK to be frightened but nothing will happen to me. My anxiety will pass if I give it time'.)

4. If you are using your coping strategies your anxiety is likely to abate and once it has reduced to, say, a three, you can choose something a little more difficult from the list you have drawn up.

> *Michelle practised this exercise for two days, three times a day until her anxiety had subsided to three. It was at this point that she decided to take a trip to her local underground station and undertake the exercise for real.*
>
> *Michelle found that the exercise went well, and although her anxiety went up to five when doing the exercise for real, it took very little time for it to subside. She used all her coping strategies and was very pleased with what she achieved. Her success gave her the confidence to increase the degree of difficulty using the items on her list. It took her only just over 10 days of regular daily practice to lose her fear of public transport.*

To gain the maximum benefit from the above technique, you need to practise it frequently. Once you feel confident enough, you need to follow through with a real life event. When you undertake a live exercise, you should use all the coping strategies you have practised in your imagination. It is also important to remember to break down your exercises into small, manageable steps. Trying to do too much will put too much strain on you and could lead to a sense of failure. Remember that old maxim '*success breeds success*'.

Medication

The most common *tranquillisers* are the valium-like drugs, the benzodiazepines (most sleeping tablets also belong to this class of drugs). They are very effective at relieving anxiety, but we now know that they can be addictive after only four weeks' regular use. When people try to stop taking them they may experience unpleasant withdrawal symptoms that can persist for some time. These drugs should be used for short periods only, perhaps to help during a crisis. They should not be used for longer-term treatment of anxiety.

On the other hand, *anti-depressants* are NOT addictive and can help to relieve anxiety as well as the depression for which they are usually prescribed. Some even seem to have a particular effect on individual types of anxiety. One of the drawbacks is that they usually take two to four weeks to work and some can cause drowsiness, dizziness, dry mouth and constipation. Taking a certain kind of anti-depressant, the monoamine oxidase inhibitors (MAOIs), may mean that you have to stick to a special diet.

Problem-solving

Being able to deal with problems can help you manage your anxiety. Your thinking style, as we saw in Chapter 3, affects how effectively you manage your life. Solving problems provides you with the chance of learning new skills. Figure 8 presents a problem-solving model comprising six stages

Stage one: identify the problem

The first step is to identify exactly what is wrong. When defining a problem it is important to be as clear and specific as possible about what exactly is troubling you.

You identify the problem by:

● writing down what is happening, who is involved and what you believe is wrong, e.g. **Situation:** *been asked*

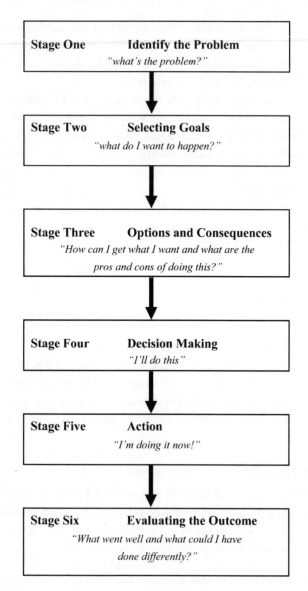

Figure 8.   The six stage problem solving model

to produce a report. **Those involved**: *two colleagues and me*. **What is wrong?**: *I don't seem to have all the information and am not sure how to get it*;

● drawing a circle in the middle of a page to represent you and then putting all the external and internal influences around you. For example, *an external influence* would be the actual information you need, whereas *an internal influence* might be *'feeling unsure of how to present the information'*.

Stage two: selecting goals

The next task is to set yourself a goal. Your goal needs to be specific. Although *'I want to produce a good report'* tells you what you want, it is not specific enough. A better alternative would be *'I want to write a report that covers all the options available to our organization'*. This example more clearly states what you want to do.

If you set yourself a goal you have to measure whether you are achieving it or not. Goals need to be specific and measurable as well as realistic. Are you one of those people who set themselves unrealistic goals? For example, *'I want to write the best report without asking anyone for their input even though I have only half the picture'*. If you set yourself unrealistic goals you are likely to be discouraged and feel like a failure.

The next step is to make sure your goal is relevant and the last part of the goal-setting process is to set yourself a time limit. Are you going to write the report in twenty-four hours, seventy-two hours, or a week?

One way of remembering the goal-making process is to remember the acronym *SMART.*

S pecific:	Goals should be short and clear
	e.g. I want to write a report that illustrates all the options available to us
M easurable:	This considers how you will measure your progress.
	e.g. I will check with all the relevant parties to ensure I get all the information I need.
A chievable:	Is your Goal realistic?
	e.g. If I use the next two days to do my research I can use the third day to make a rough draft and the fourth to complete the task.
R elevant:	How relevant is my Goal?
	e.g it will be helpful to my career to write a good report particularly as this is the first I have been asked to write.
T ime:	How much time should I allocate?
	e.g. I will have the task completed by Friday, which provides me with an extra day for any unexpected difficulties.

Stage three: options and consequences

OPTIONS

Once you have identified the problem you need to consider the associated consequences.

Brainstorming

Brainstorming is one technique you can use to help you expand your options. Brainstorming involves:

1. Writing down the issue at the top of the page.

2. Giving yourself ten minutes to come up with as many ideas as you can. As you write down your ideas you:
   - do not censor your ideas, regardless of how far fetched you think they are
   - go for quantity and not quality at this stage.
3. Once you have exhausted yourself in terms of your ideas, you can go back over them and see which ones seem useful and which ones you will disregard.

Who can help you?

Perhaps you know someone who has dealt with a similar situation – how did they do it? If your problem is work-related perhaps your organization offers a coaching scheme. If your problem is personal you may have a friend or family member who can help.

CONSEQUENCES

Now that you have identified your options you need to consider the pros and cons attached to each one. As in the cost–benefits analysis earlier, it is best to write everything down.

Brainstorming is a good tool for considering the consequences of a particular course of action. In an earlier chapter you were introduced to the power of imagery and using your imagination. You may wish to visualize your options and use your imagination to 'see' what could happen.

Stage four: decision making

Your plan may require one course of action or a series of actions. If you are unable to make a decision it may be because:

- It is impossible to solve the problem – maybe all that can be done is to manage the situation.
- You may need more information.
- You may be unclear about choosing between the various options available to you.

If you believe the problem is impossible to solve try rewording it or breaking it down into smaller sections that are more easily resolved. If you require more information, you need to decide how to get this.

When you are confused between two or more options you may find it useful to talk to a friend or colleague. Use the rating scale (0–10) you were introduced to earlier to see if any of the options has the edge over another. Think about each option and try to visualize how you imagine things would be if you took that course of action.

How to manage setbacks

Although you have considered the pros and cons of a variety of actions you may also find it useful to have a contingency plan worked out. A contingency plan means thinking about what to do if things do not go according to plan.

For example, if you wanted to write a report what could get in the way of your completing it? How many things could go wrong and how would you react to each of them? The following example of a personal contingency plan is a way of helping you think through and predict all the things that could go wrong, and how you would deal with such events if they occurred. Brainstorm as many problems as you can foresee before undertaking this exercise.

PERSONAL CONTINGENCY PLAN
Feeling (rate 0–10)

What could go wrong?	What could I do if this happens?
1. I might not have enough time to write the report	1. I need to make out a timetable
2. I might not get the information I need	2. I need to make an outline of all the headings and then make a note of where I will obtain the information
3. My feelings of anxiety might get the better of me	3. If I use my breathing exercises and challenge my cognitions I will be able to manage my feelings
4.	4.
5.	5.
6.	6.

You may find that some of your plans of action require practice, for example, practising challenging unhelpful cognitions.

Stage five: action

Once you have made your decision you need to ensure that you are fully resourced with everything you need to take action. You may find it helpful to keep a note of every action you take with its outcome. By completing an action plan you can tick off everything you have completed and see how each of your actions adds up to changing your situation. Some people find it helpful to place a series of reminders or Post-it notes around the house, office, in a diary and/or on the telephone. These Post-it notes act as reminders for the things that need to be done.

Example

17 November 2003

1. Ring John and ask him for a copy of the last report so I can see what it is like as it may help me with the one I am writing.
2. Remember to practise my breathing exercise as this helps me stay calm.

Stage six: evaluating the outcome

You are the best judge of whether your problem is solved. Using the SMART goal-setting formula mentioned earlier makes it easier to measure your success. By making your goal specific it is easier to see how far you have gone in achieving what you set out to do. Another way is to use what is called a 'continuum'; that is a line that acts as a graded scale of how far you feel you have managed to come. Once you have drawn your line, place your X at the point that you believe most closely matches your progress.

Example

Not writing the report————X————completed report

If you have achieved what you set out to do then you can bring the problem-solving process to an end. If you have made no progress at all you need to radically over-haul the steps you have taken and the decisions you have made. You may, for example, have been rather ambitious in the goal you set yourself. It may have seemed feasible at the time but you may have found the implementation more difficult than you anticipated. If this is the case, you need to go back to the beginning of the problem-solving process and, this time, break down the tasks into more manageable steps.

You may have identified more deep-rooted problems that you feel you cannot tackle on your own and you may require professional help. On those occasions where a partial completion of goals has been achieved, you need to consider what went well and what proved difficult. You may feel you are happy enough with what you have achieved or you may feel that you need to take those aspects that you have been less successful with and set about a new problem-solving process with these.

Assertion training

Assertion training encourages people to use skills that build upon inner resources. Assertiveness aids clear communication with other people.

Assertiveness quiz

The following questions are designed to help you assess your behaviour patterns. Be honest in your responses and answer each question by writing in your notebook the most appropriate answer: '**Yes**', '**No**', '**Sometimes**' or '**Never**'. Choose the response that most closely matches your behaviour.

1. Do you say what you feel?
2. Do you make decisions easily?
3. Are you critical of other people?
4. Do you say something if someone pushes in front of you?

5. Do you usually have confidence in your own decision-making capacity?
6. Do you lose your temper quickly?
7. Do you find it hard to say 'No'
8. Do you continue with an argument after the other
   person has finished?
9. When you discover goods are faulty, do you take
   them back?
10. Do you feel shy in social situations?
11. Are you able to show your emotions?
12. Are you able to ask people for help?

Note: There is no right or wrong answer to the questions
above. The answers you have given provide you with
information about your personal style of behaviour. You
are now in a position to decide whether you are happy
with the answers you have given and whether you would
like to change the way that you behave.

Four types of behaviour

Non-assertive/passive

PERSONAL FEELINGS

A non-assertive person often feels helpless, powerless,
inadequate, frustrated and lacking in confidence.

Behaviours

Signs of being passive:

- not asking for what you want;
- not saying what you feel;

- avoiding situations where you have to make decisions'
- feeling like a victim and/or martyr;
- finding it hard to say 'no' so you become over-committed and frustrated.

How others feel

Being around a non-assertive person can leave others feeling frustrated. You could feel sorry for the person at first but then, having tried to help him/her and, in some cases having received no response you end up feeling irritated and annoyed.

Consequences

Non-assertive people avoid taking responsibility and risks. They want to avoid rejection and the decision-making process. Many people who suffer from anxiety are often passive.

Aggressive

PERSONAL FEELINGS

Aggressive people often feel out of control. Although they may feel superior in the short-term they may also feel fearful, insecure, and suffer from a lack of confidence.

Exercise

Write down the following words, then circle those that best describe you.

Helpless	Powerless	Inadequate
Frustrated	Victim	Martyr
Over-committed	Poor confidence	
Avoids risks	Avoids rejection	

Signs of aggression

- You shout, bully, and use verbal and/or physical force to get your own way.
- You feel you must 'win' at all costs and anything except getting your own way is 'failure'.
- You do not respect the rights of other people.

How others feel

Aggressive behaviour can lead people to feel scared, angry, helpless, and used.

Consequences

Aggressive people tend to dominate. Their aggressive behaviour means they do not need to explain, negotiate, or listen to others. However, in the longer term an aggressive person may become isolated and lose the respect of others.

Exercise

Write down the following words, then circle those that best describe you.

Shouts	Hits objects	Bullies others
Wags finger	Superior	Fearful
Insecure	Poor confidence	

Indirectly aggressive/passive–aggressive

PERSONAL FEELINGS

When you behave in a passive–aggressive manner you may feel frustrated, disappointed, and lacking in confidence.

Signs of indirectly aggressive/passive–aggressive behaviours

- You are unpredictable. One day you agree and the next you disagree about the same subject.
- You hold grudges and bide your time to pay back others.
- You sulk and are able to generate a difficult atmosphere around you.

How others feel

When someone is around a passive–aggressive person they may find themselves feeling angry, hurt, confused, manipulated, and guilty.

Consequences

This type of behaviour is aimed at avoiding direct confrontation and rejection and often leads to a breakdown in relationships.

Exercise

Write down the following words and circle those that best describe you.

Frustrated   Disappointed Lacking in confidence
Holds grudges Pay-back   Sulking
Avoids confrontation

Assertive

PERSONAL FEELINGS

An assertive person often feels relaxed and confident. Assertiveness does not provide immunity against experiencing difficult emotions and an assertive person has a full

99

range of emotions. However, an assertive person can choose the appropriate behaviour to use.

Signs of assertiveness

- I ask for what I want.
- I attempt to be clear in what I say.
- I listen to the needs of others.
- I respect myself and other people.
- I aim for 'win–win' situations and am happy to compromise without seeing compromising as something negative.

How others react

Those who are around an assertive person will usually feel valued, respected, and listened to. An assertive person's behaviour makes people feel safe, secure, and fairly treated.

Consequences

Assertive people seize opportunities, develop healthy relationships, and feel genuinely confident.

Exercise

Write down the following words and circle those that best describe you.

Confident Relaxed Listens to others Win–win
Seizes opportunities Respects others Respects self

What assertiveness involves

Respect for self and for others

Assertive people respect themselves and other people equally. They choose to show this respect in the way they openly, honestly, and genuinely deal with other people. They will stand up for themselves. Setting boundaries is one way in which we show respect for ourselves. It is up to each individual to decide what boundaries to create.

For example: '*I appreciate that you want me to babysit for you tomorrow. However, I had made alternative plans and would be happy to sit another night.*'

Taking personal responsibility for thoughts, feelings, and actions

Assertive people are prepared to take responsibility for what they say, for what they feel, and for what they do. They realize how important it is to act in a responsible way.

For example: '*I feel put down when you shout at me*' is more assertive than '*You make me angry when you shout at me*'. Using the word 'I' is one way of taking responsibility for what you feel, think, say, and do – for example, '*I feel let down about this decision*'.

Recognizing and making choices

Assertive people recognize the need to make choices and do not avoid doing so. They believe that even if they make the wrong choice it is not the end of the world. Assertiveness means taking risks and assertive people believe that life is based on acceptable risk-taking.

Some assertiveness skills

The three steps to assertiveness

STEP ONE

Listen to what the other person is saying and demonstrate you have *heard* and *understood* what has been said. You are more likely to get the outcome you seek if the other person feels you have really heard him/her. Very often we are more concerned with what we want to say than what the other person has said, and this can lead to the pantomime situation of '*Oh yes you did, oh no, I didn't*'.

Charles: *I felt cross at the way you spoke to me in front of other people.*

John: *I can see that you could have felt cross with me.*

STEP TWO

In step two you say what you *think* or *feel*. If this stage is to flow smoothly you need to use a *link* word or phrase such as 'however', or 'on the other hand', or 'alternatively'.

John: *However, you did say that we should speak up at team meetings if we had a proble*m.

STEP THREE

In step three you say what you *want to happen*. To help this section flow from the one before you need to use the link word *and*. In step three you are looking for what could be called a workable compromise, something that will sort the situation out and help both parties learn something useful for the next time such a situation arises.

John: *And perhaps we could work out how we manage this kind of situation for next time.*

Example

Step one:	*'I understand you want me to change my holiday plans.'*
Link word:	*However*
Step two:	*'I have my wife to consider as we have already set the dates.'*
Link word:	*and*
Step three:	*'I need to talk to her first before I can give you an answer.'*

Managing instant reactions

Change takes time. If you find yourself reacting quickly count to three in your head and take a deep breath. This should slow you down so that you can make a more considered response.

Less is more

You may find you over-explain yourself in the answers you give. If this is the case try to keep what you say short and simple. After all, you can have more than one bite of the apple and do not have to say everything in one go.

More assertiveness skills

Broken record

There will be times when you have used the three-step model and the person seems to ignore what you say. In this case, you need to repeat what you have said in a consistent way until your message cannot be ignored. The idea is to restate the essence of what you are saying rather than always using the same words.

Example

Jamie: *I appreciate you want me to make a decision. However, I need to think about the situation first and suggest I come back to you with an answer by the end of the week.*

Mike: *It's not that big a deal. Surely you can say yes or no now?*

Jamie: *I can understand it is frustrating for you. However, I do need to think about things and then come back to you.*

Negative feelings assertion

You need to identify the behaviour that troubles you, explain how it affects you, and say what you want to happen. For example, if someone is shouting at you, you may find it hard to listen to what is being said and you can say so. If the person is sulking, you may feel that you cannot get through to him/her to sort out what is wrong and this damages your feelings towards that person.

Example

'*I feel irritated when you raise your voice* (the behaviour) *and find it really hard to listen to what you have to say* (how it affects you) *and I do want to be able to help you* (what you want to happen).'

Workable compromise

This works on the basis of finding a solution that both of you can live with. It's about aiming for a 'win–win' situation, and it means both of you compromising. People who aim to communicate in this way increase their bank of goodwill as they see goodwill as a kind of investment that can be called upon later.

Example

Irene: *Everyone will be there. You just have to come.*
June: *I know there will be a lot of people. However, it's not really something I would enjoy and maybe we could arrange one of our nights out for the week after.*
Irene: *I guess that's fair.*

Deflecting

Deflecting can be used to diffuse aggressive situations. It is based on the principle that no one is perfect and requires you only to agree that the person making the statement has a right to his or her own point of view. If you agree with the person you are not selling out – just simply acknowledging their right to their own view. Most people are waiting for us to disagree with them and all this disagreement gains is a game of '*oh yes you did*', '*oh no I didn't*'. If you agree with part of what is being said you can stop the situation from escalating.

Example

Gary: *You always seem to know what's right and never seem to think other people might have a point.*
        (This sort of statement could easily lead to a row.)
Delia: *You may have a point. It wouldn't be my intention to come across like that but I guess it's possible that I do* (by agreeing only to the possibility you act in a way which is non-defensive and defuses a potentially explosive situation).

Discrepancy assertion

This skill simply requires you to highlight any inconsistencies in what is being said.

Example

'*On the one hand you say you really dislike your job and on the other you say you have lots of interesting things to do.*'

Thinking it over time

Changing behaviour takes time. If you have been someone who says 'yes' without thinking, you may find yourself continuing to do so. One way of breaking the cycle is to ask for thinking it over time. When asked something, take time to consider your position. If you are on the telephone, suggest that you ring the person back at a certain time – '*I can't speak now so let me ring you back in twenty minutes*'.

If you are actually with someone, you can say, '*I need time to think about what you have said*'.

A quick trip to the loo is an effective way to buy time. A quick '*excuse me*' followed by a few minutes taking time to think about what you want to say can provide the space you need to make a sensible decision.

Your personal rights

These rights are a way to get you thinking about how you value yourself. Alongside rights are also the responsibilities we have towards others. Assertiveness means respecting self and others equally. You do not have the right to infringe the rights of others and you give yourself the same rights you give other people.

Exercise

Consider the following statements and ask yourself whether you agree or disagree with them.

Agree/Disagree

- I have the right to be treated with respect as an equal human being.
- I have the right to ask for what I want.
- I have the right to look after my needs and say 'No'.
- I have the right to express my feelings and thoughts.
- I have the right to ask for time before making a decision.
- I have the right to make my own decisions.
- I have the right to change my mind.
- I have the right to refuse responsibility for other people's problems if I so choose.
- I have the right to choose not to be assertive.

Exercise

Write down in your notebook any other rights you want to add to those above.

Dealing with difficult situations

Coping with conflict

No one gets through life without having to face conflict situations. Most people dislike conflict but many of us make the situation worse by the way we deal with it. Anxious people often avoid conflict and then feel put upon or not valued.

Assertiveness skills provide you with a set of skills to deal with what is said so that you can verbally influence a positive outcome.

Work towards a win–win outcome

Try to think about what you want and what you think the other person might want. See if you can give the other person something of what they want as this is more likely to make them amenable and get you more of what you want with the least amount of hassle.

Separate yourself and the other person from the issue

When the temperature rises and when you want something, emotions such as anxiety can get in the way. Strong emotions block the ability to listen and think – both of which are required if conflict is to be resolved without damaging the relationship.

Take responsibility and make clear 'I' statements

You are responsible for your own thoughts and actions. If you want to handle conflict assertively you need to ensure you make clear 'I' statements as a way of demonstrating your needs and wants.

One issue at a time and know what you want to happen

Your conflict with a person may be about one issue or it may be about many issues. You might find you have bottled things up and that there is a danger of too many subjects being talked about at the same time. Successful conflict resolution means dealing with one subject at a time. This means making a list of all the things you want to talk about and then deciding which one to discuss first.

Give your undivided attention

You are far more likely to get a positive outcome if you can demonstrate your respect for the other person by the way you deal with them.

The right time and the right place

If you really want to resolve a situation, then think about when and where you are going to deal with it. There is also little point in trying to resolve conflict if you are likely to be disturbed or in a crowded place. Choose a private location and time when both of you are free.

Dealing with requests

There are times when people will ask you to do something for them. If you are happy to say yes then fine. However, many people say yes when they really want to say no. There are four steps for dealing with requests.

Step one: what do you feel?

Many people override their basic 'gut' reaction to a request and some people not only override it, they also don't notice it. When someone makes a request, you may find yourself feeling uncomfortable in some way. If this is the case ask yourself what you feel uncomfortable about. It may also help you to ask yourself the following questions.

Do I feel used in some way?
Do I feel 'I have to' and, if so, why?
What's the worse that could happen if I say no?
What feeling am I experiencing (anger, fear, embarrassment etc.)?

Step two: saying 'no'

If you want to say 'no', say so clearly. It is perfectly reasonable to provide an explanation but don't excuse or justify yourself. If you over-explain it usually means you feel bad about saying no and are trying to justify your position.

Step three: saying 'yes'

If you want to say 'yes', say so clearly. If you are happy to say yes but want to modify what you are prepared to offer then outline the conditions that apply.

Step four: not sure

If you are not sure what you want:

- Ask for more information to help you make your decision.
- Ask for more time to consider your decision.
- Suggest a compromise if you believe this is appropriate.
- Watch out for an 'indirect no' – a way of trying to avoid saying no by stating things in ways that are

aimed at getting the other person to take back the request.

Handling criticism

Many people believe that criticism means they are inadequate in some way or are being unfairly targeted, as mentioned earlier.

You can handle criticism by:

- Being clear about what the criticism is about. Ask for more information.
- Asking for more time to consider what has been said. After all, it can be difficult to identify what you think or feel immediately.
- Asking for more information, if required, and then stating clearly your need for time to consider what has been said. Wherever possible tell the person when you will come back to him/her.
- Once you have thought about what has been said you need to decide whether you think the criticism is valid or not. If you agree with what has been said, you need to accept the criticism and discuss any future changes. If you disagree with what has been said. then ensure you disagree confidently, making sure you do not apologise.

Giving criticism

Giving criticism can be as hard for some people as receiving it, especially for people who suffer from anxiety. Holding on to negative feelings doesn't help. If you are a manager you will have to give criticism to your staff at some time or another. If you are a parent you will have to criticize your children from time to time, otherwise they may never learn and could go on to develop unhelpful ways of relating to others.

You can give criticism effectively by:

- Finding a private place to have the discussion. If you want someone to think about what you are saying you need to respect his or her feelings.
- Find something good to say about the person's behaviour. Acknowledge the person's good points as well as bad points. Be genuine in what you say.
- Try to avoid becoming too personal. Keep your comments to the facts of the situation and how you feel.
- Criticize the person's behaviour. Behaviour is something you have control over whereas there may be things about yourself you cannot change, for example, whether you speak with an accent.
- Describe your feelings and how you are affected by the person's behaviour.
- Make sure you listen to what the other person has to say. Effective communication requires active participation and active listening.
- The other person needs to understand the consequence of not changing. If someone knows that a particular behaviour upsets you or damages your relationship, this can be enough to motivate him or her to change.

Managing put-downs

There are a number of different ways in which people may try to put you down, and some of these are listed below.

Making decisions for you

Trying to make a decision for you puts you down as it takes away your personal responsibility. If this is the case you need to let the person know you are capable of making your own decisions, for example, '*I appreciate you have my best interests at heart. However, I need to do this myself.*'

Putting the pressure on you

Sometimes people drop something on us when we are least expecting it as a way of trying to force us to make a decision or go along with what they are saying. This type of action puts you on the spot. If this is the case you need to ask for time to think about what's being asked of you.

Making claims that you are lying

A person may suggest directly or indirectly that what you have said is not true, the implication being that you are lying. If this is the case you need to be clear about what you are saying. For example, '*It is my understanding that Jane was the last person to leave the office.*'

WHAT AN ANXIETY-FREE
LIFE REQUIRES

You have the skills to improve the way you interact with other people, influencing a more positive outcome for yourself, although there are still some common areas of concern that you need to consider before you can really say you live an anxiety-free life.

Time management

If you are unable to manage your time effectively you will not follow through on the promises you make yourself to improve your life. You might find yourself wanting and wishing things to be different but saying you don't have enough time to practise your new skills.

Time is a valuable commodity. How many times do you catch yourself saying, '*I'd want to but don't have the time*' or '*There really does seem too much to do*'. Too much activity leads to exhaustion; too little and you could become bored and frustrated. There are 168 hours in a week and 8,760 hours in a 365-day year, and so with a finite amount of time it is important that you make the most of what you have. Try the following exercise to see how much of your time daily activities absorb.

Exercise

To help you consider your time management needs, think about the activities you are involved in on a weekly basis and list these in a copy of the table below.

ITEM   TIME ALLOCATION

---

e.g. Family commitments

Travel

How effectively do you allocate your time?

Ask yourself the following questions.

1. Do I have time to do what I would like to?   Yes/No
2. Do I put off activities because I have   Yes/No
   too much to do?
3. Do I feel there simply is not enough time?   Yes/No
4. Have I ever thought about the way I use
   my time?   Yes/No
5. Am I happy about the way I allocate   Yes/No
   my time?

If you have answered yes to questions 2 and 3 and no to questions 1, 4, and 5, you might need to consider how you allocate your time and whether this is effective for you.

Time can be divided into six areas and it may be helpful to draw a circle, labelling this your 'Time Allowance Pie' (see Figure 9). Consider each of the six areas below and divide your pie into the portions that you believe accurately represents your allocation of time over a one-week period (see also pp. 23–24).

Work time: time earmarked for work, paid or voluntary.

Home time: time for housework/maintenance, personal care, and gardening.

'Other' time: time for family, friends and children.

'Me' time: time for hobbies, relaxation, exercise and sleep.

'Us' time: time to spend with our partner.

Quiet time: time to ourselves for thinking, evaluating and reflecting (*e.g. how well you are doing at learning to be your own life coach*).

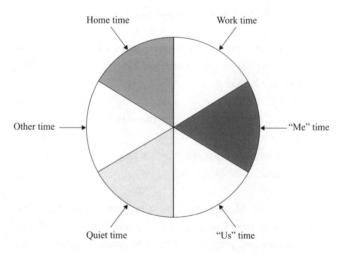

Figure 9. Time allocation pie

If you are not happy with the amount of time you have allocated to any activity consider how to reallocate the time you have so that you achieve the balance you are seeking. If there are slices of your pie that are greatly out of balance you may find it helpful to keep a written record of your feelings about how you have allocated your time over a one week period.

Apart from completing the time allocation pie you could also consider:

1. How you manage your time.
2. How you fritter your time away.
3. How you could be more effective in managing your time.
4. How you could make more time to do the things you like.
5. How you could do less of the things you dislike.

At the end of a week you should have a better idea of how you spend your time and what you would like to create more or less time to do.

Your biological clock has an effect on time management, as there are times of the day when you will feel more alert than others. For example, some people prefer mornings, when they feel full of energy, but find they feel exhausted by mid-afternoon. If this is the case, it makes sense to try, wherever possible, to save your difficult tasks for the time of the day when you have most energy. Your best time of day is often called your 'prime time'.

Consider other people's 'prime time' as there may be times of the day when it would be better to approach certain people. If there are times of the day when you are more energetic why not seek out such times in others, as this may help influence a positive outcome.

There are three aspects of time management to consider:

- Checklists and notes as ways of keeping track of the work you have to do.
- Calendars and appointment books for planning ahead.
- Short-, medium- and long-term goal setting and the recognition of your personal values and desires.

Poor organization

Poor organization can mean

- poorly maintained filing system (*e.g., filing not done on a regular basis*). Valuable time can be lost looking for information.
- no system to identify relevant information (*e.g., papers and documentation simply thrown into a pile*)
- indiscriminately keeping everything that is received, filling valuable space as well as using time to locate items – the 'just in case' principle.

If you find yourself spending time on non-productive discussions either at work or with friends when you need to be doing something else, consider the following:

- keep conversations short;
- keep a clock nearby to remind you to deal with the call effectively;
- learn how to use the three step model of assertiveness.

Step 1: I understand your problem: e.g., '*I do appreciate you need to meet with me*'
Step 2: However, I think or feel: *e.g.*, '*However, I need to do some research*'

Step 3: and I suggest: e.g., '*and I suggest we speak at the end of the week when I have all the information*'.

Diaries, personal and electronic organizers

A diary or a personal or electronic organizer are mechanisms to keep track of appointments and are good for planning ahead. If you use a diary or personal organizer you may also find it useful to mark your appointments in pencil, as this allows them to be changed with the minimum of fuss. If you choose to use an electronic organizer you need to back up your data on a regular basis to protect against loss of information.

'To do' lists

A 'to do' list is a form of memory aid. In addition to recording tasks to be done, a simple system such as A, B and C can be used as a way of organizing priorities.

A = **Urgent items** which require immediate attention.
B = **Important items** which require attention in the near future.
C = **Non-essential or non-urgent items**.

Post-it notes

Some people find it helpful to place post-it notes in full view to remind them to carry out urgent tasks.

Filing systems

A portable, lockable metal filing system can prove useful to help you store household documentation. Being able to find something first time can really save you time.

Effective time management means thinking about what you do, how you do it, and how you can make the most of this finite resource. Unlike most items, time cannot be stored for future use.

To ensure you use your time effectively you need to build in 'quiet' time as a legitimate activity. This type of activity enables you to evaluate the present while considering the future.

Stress busting

Stress involves a complex relationship between the demands made of a person and the personal and external resources he or she has to meet these demands.

The demands that are made of you could be 'internal', that is your own thinking style. Perfectionists put pressure on themselves and this is therefore an internal demand as no one else is making it. Resources comprise factors such as your physical health, financial security, social and family support. Keep a balance so you do not have more demands than resources to deal with them. If demands exceed your resources you may feel you cannot cope and this is the beginning of what has become known as stress.

Some people talk about healthy and unhealthy stress, meaning that some stress is good for you. It is easier to think in terms of the idea of 'pressure' and 'stress'. Pressure is healthy and something that can motivate you. Some people love to live in a pressured way with lots of deadlines and things to do. The distinction between pressure and stress is that you experience pressure when you have the resources you need to deal with the demands being made of you. Pressure turns to stress when the pressure becomes too great, lasts too long, comes suddenly, and ends up with you feeling that it cannot be controlled.

Stress is a very personal matter. A situation that might stress your friend may not affect you and vice versa. An event may have proved stressful to you at one point in your life but you may have developed additional resources to deal with the situation as you have grown older.

Work can be a great source of stress – time pressures, excessive workload, poor relations with colleagues/managers, poor communications within your organization, being exposed to continual change, not being trained to do the job, and job insecurity all play their part. Stress can be experienced in your personal life – family problems, life changes/crises, increasing demands between home and work – all may affect us.

In 1967, Thomas Holmes and Richard Rahe, two American psychologists, first published a scale of forty-three life events considered to be stressful. Each event was scored according to the degree of stress associated with the activity. Listed below are the top seven items together with the score associated with each event.

The life event	Score
Death of a partner	100
Divorce	73
Marital separation	65
Imprisonment	63
Death of a close family member	63
Personal illness or injury	53
Marriage	50

In addition to the above, other items included:

- Dealing with Christmas.
- Pregnancy.
- Sexual difficulties.
- Legal action.
- Moving house.
- Changing school or college.
- Change in living conditions.
- Change in hours or working conditions.
- Arguments with partners or family.
- Adoption or birth of a child.

One of the advantages of understanding the impact of life events is that it can help you anticipate stressful events. For example, knowing that having a baby can be stressful allows you to consider what stress management techniques are likely to help you. A fact that surprised many people was that life events seen as pleasurable also carried a stress rating, for example, getting married, having a baby, or gaining a promotion. Good experiences usually entail a degree of change and it can be the changes to lifestyle and the need to develop new coping skills that contribute to the stress experienced.

THE ANXIETY-FREE DIET

Anxiety and dietary tips

Anxiety can be made worse by taking stimulants such as tea, coffee, colas, and chocolate, all of which contain caffeine. Caffeine is a stimulant and stimulants are best avoided when we are experiencing emotions such as anxiety. Because we produce adrenaline when we are feeling anxious, this can affect our blood sugar levels and they may indeed drop dramatically. Therefore, in order to keep those levels balanced, it is important to eat 'little and often' during the day. It may also be helpful to avoid refined sugars and other substances which 'give too much of a high' too quickly. Slow-release foods such as carbohydrates (potatoes, pasta, rice, bread, apples and bananas) are a much better idea as they fuel the body in a more even, controlled way.

These days it is impossible to avoid information on healthy eating. However, what we eat also has an effect on our confidence levels and our ability to cope emotionally.

As was outlined in the Stress Busting chapter above, our bodies produce stress hormones and release fatty acids and sugars to help us cope with a perceived crisis. When such events take place our bodies' natural blood sugar levels are disturbed and this is also the case when we become angry or anxious. Our blood sugars help us regulate the fuel requirements needed by our body. Low blood sugar or hypoglycaemia contributes to symptoms of anxiety.

A drop in blood sugar causes reactions in the nervous system, including feelings of anxiety, confusion and panic attacks. Diets that contain large amounts of refined sugars or are deficient in protein or fat together with the use of stimulants such as coffee or cola based drinks contribute to this condition.

Vitamin and mineral deficiencies also contribute to feelings of anxiety. You may be lacking in magnesium, zinc and the amino acid tryptophan. Alternatively, an excessive amount of some nutrients can speed up your nervous system and this can lead to feelings of anxiety. Potassium, sodium, phosphorus, and copper are just such minerals.

If the thyroid or adrenal glands become overactive, such conditions affect the way we feel as we cannot absorb and use sufficient minerals and, as a result, anxiety may follow. An underactive thyroid is more likely to lead to feelings of depression than of anxiety.

What can I do to help myself?

If you have any concerns at all about your health, your first port of call should be your doctor. I have always believed that all medical conditions should be eliminated before considering any emotional and/or life factors.

The following are some dietary tips that will help you:

- Drink plenty of water – not only is it good for your skin, it helps flush out toxins and keeps your kidneys in good working order. Around eight large glasses a day is best. There is nothing wrong with flavouring the water if you are not keen on drinking water. However, avoid sugary flavourings as this will defeat the object. Drinking fruit teas are also a good way of getting water inside you.

- Make sure you eat at least six times a day. Breakfast, mid-morning, lunch, mid-afternoon, tea, and dinner. By eating little and often and ensuring you do not skip meals you will help your blood sugar levels stay balanced.

- Keep healthy snacks around you and plan ahead for days when it may be difficult to find healthy meals.

- Try to avoid 'fast food' as it usually contains more fat and additives than are good for you.

- Take a multivitamin pill daily. It can be difficult to ensure you get all the nutrients you need through the food you eat and a multivitamin will help ensure you are topped up on any you may be missing.

- Try to avoid coffee, tea, cola drinks, and chocolate, as all these contain varying amounts of caffeine. It would be a sad world if you could not allow yourself a little of what you fancy, so if you want chocolate now and again buy the more expensive kind, which has a higher concentration of cocoa solids and less sugar.

- Try to avoid saturated fats as these can lead to health problems. A diet that is high in fat will also contain high levels of cholesterol. There is an increased risk of cancer of the breast, colon, and prostate as well as coronary heart disease.

- Try to avoid an excess of alcohol – it dehydrates, is a depressant, and can increase mood-swings and depressive symptoms, and fuel aggression.

- Avoid excessive amounts of salt (sodium) as about a quarter of what we require is to be found naturally present in food. We require so little that we can quite happily survive on what occurs in our daily food.

What food can I eat?

The aim is to eat as varied a diet as possible. However, the following will provide you with a more detailed breakdown of a range of foods that contribute to good physical as well as psychological health.

Protein

- Meat, chicken
- Fish, shellfish
- Dried beans
- Soya products

Carbohydrates

COMPLEX

- Wholegrain bread
- Pasta
- Rice
- Peas and beans
- Vegetables
- Fruit and nuts

REFINED SUGAR (NOT SO HELPFUL)

- Sweet foods

Calcium

- Milk, cheese, yoghurt
- Fish
- Broccoli, spring greens, leeks, cabbage, parsnips, potatoes, blackberries, oranges

Potassium

- Potatoes and sweet potatoes
- Fish, sardines
- Pork, chicken
- Cauliflower, sweetcorn, avocados, leeks
- Breakfast cereals
- Natural yoghurt
- Bananas, rhubarb

Iron

- Egg

WHAT TYPE OF HELP IS AVAILABLE?

The Royal College of Psychiatrists has recommended a number of ways in which an individual can seek help.

Talking about the problem

This can help when the anxiety comes from recent knocks, like a spouse leaving, a child becoming ill, or losing a job. Who should we talk to? Try friends or relatives whom you trust, whose opinions you respect, and who are good listeners. They may have had the same problem themselves, or know someone else who has. As well as having the chance to talk, we may be able to find out how other people have coped with a similar problem.

Self-help groups

These are a good way of getting in touch with people with similar problems. They will be able to understand what you are going through, and may also be able to suggest helpful ways of coping. These groups may be focused on anxieties and phobias, or may be made up of people who have been through similar experiences – women's groups, bereaved parent's groups, survivors of abuse groups.

Learning to relax

It can be a great help to learn a special way of relaxing, to help control anxiety and tension. Such techniques can be learnt through groups or through professionals, but there are also several teach yourself books and videotapes (see below). It's a good idea to practise these regularly, not just when we are in a crisis situation.

Psychotherapy

This is a more intensive talking treatment that can help people to understand and to come to terms with reasons for their anxieties that they may not have recognized themselves. The treatment can take place in groups or individually and is usually weekly for several weeks or months. Psychotherapists may or may not be medically qualified.

If this is not enough, there are several different kinds of professionals who may be able to help – the family doctor, psychiatrist, psychologist, social worker, nurse, or counsellor.

Medication

Drugs can play a part in the treatment of some people with anxiety or phobias.

FURTHER READING

Overcoming Panic
Derrick Silove and Vijaya Manicavasagar (Robinson Publishing Ltd)

Overcoming Social Anxiety and Shyness
Gillian Butler (Robinson Publishing Ltd)

Overcoming Anxiety
Helen Kennerley (Robinson Publishing Ltd)

USEFUL RESOURCES

Alcohol Concern
Waterbridge House
32-36 Loman Street
London SE1 OEE
Tel: 0207 928 7377
Provides information on alcohol and its effects and can provide details of alcohol agencies, residential, advice and drop-in, across the UK.

Alzheimer's Society
Gordon House
10 Greencoat Place
London SW1P 1PH
Tel: 020 7306 0606
Helpline: 0845 300 0336
www.alzheimers.org.uk
Information and support for carers; campaigns, research.

Association for Rational Emotive Behaviour Therapists
St George's
Winter Street
Sheffield S3 7ND
Tel: 0114 271 6926
www.rebt.bizland.com
Professional body for therapists using Rational Emotive Behaviour Therapy that can provide details of therapists.

Brake (Trauma Advisory Services – TAS)
PO Box 272
Dorking
Surrey RH4 4FR
Tel: 01306 741113

www.brake.org.uk
Provides information, advice and guidance for those
involved in trauma following road traffic accidents.

British Association for Counselling and Psychotherapy
1 Regent Place
Rugby
Warwickshire CV21 2PJ
Tel: 0788 578 328
www.counselling.co.uk
Professional body for counsellors and psychotherapists in
the UK who can provide lists of therapists as well as information and advice on counselling.

British Association for Behavioural and Cognitive Psychotherapies
PO Box 9
Accrington BB5 2GD
Tel: 01254 875277
www.babcp.com
Professional body for psychiatrists, psychologists, counsellors and all those who use cognitive–behavioural techniques. Can provide lists of therapists and also
information on cognitive–behavioural psychotherapies.

British Psychological Society
St Andrew's House
48 Princess Road East
Leicester LE1 7DR.
Tel: 0116 254 9568
www.bps.org.uk
Professional body for psychologists that can also provide
details of psychologists.

Carers National Association
20 Glasshouse Yard
London EC1A 4JS
Tel. 0207 490 8818
Carersline – advice line for carers at the cost of a local call:
0345 573 369
Association that provides help, advice and support to
those who care for others.

Centre for Stress Management
156 Westcombe Hill
Blackheath
London SE3 7DH.
Tel: 0208 293 4114
www.managingstress.com
Provides information and advice on stress related issues
together with counselling and psychotherapy. Also offers
training in a variety of subjects including stress and post
trauma stress to a range of professionals.

Child Bereavement Trust
Tel: 01628 488101
Dedicated information and support line 0845 357 1000
www.childbereavement.org.uk
Offers information, advice, and support to anyone who has
experienced the death of a child and for bereaved children.

Child Traumatic Stress Clinic
Michael Rutter Centre for Children and Adolescents
Maudsley Hospital
Denmark Hill
London
SE5 8AZ

Tel: 020 7919 2546
www.slam.nhs.uk
Offers counselling, advice and support to parents and to children who have experienced traumatic events.

COSCA (Confederation of Scottish Counselling Agencies)
18 Viewfield Street
Stirling FK8 IUE
Tel: 01786 476140
www.cosca.org.uk
Professional body for counsellors in Scotland that can provide details of counsellors and information on counselling and counselling services.

CRUSE Bereavement Care
Cruse House
126 Sheen Road
Richmond
Surrey TW9 1UR
Tel: 0208 940 4818
www.crusebereavementcare.org.uk
Offers information, advice and counselling to those who have been bereaved with local branch offices across the country.

Compassionate Friends
53 North Street
Bristol BS3 1EN
Tel: 0117 966 5202
Helpline: 08451 23 23 04
www.tcf.org.uk
Organization offering advice, counselling and support to those who have been bereaved with local branches across the country.

Divorce Conciliation and Advisory Service
38 Ebury Street
London SW1W OLU
Tel: 0207 730 2422
Provides information, advice, counselling and support.

Drinkline (The National Alcohol Helpline)
Petersham House
57 Hatton Garden
London EC1N 8HP
Tel: 0345 320202
Offers advice, counselling and support to all those with alcohol-related problems.

DrugScope
Waterbridge House
32–36 Loman Street
London SE1 0EE
Tel: 020 7928 1211
www.drugscope.org.uk
Provides information on drug misuse and details of services across the country.

Ex-Services Mental Welfare Society (also known as Combat Stress)
Tyewhitt House
Oaklawn Road
Leatherhead
Surrey KT22 OBX
Tel: 01372 841600
www.combatstress
Provides information, advice, counselling and support.

Families Need Fathers
134 Curtain Road
London EC2A 3AR
Tel: 0207 613 5060
www.fnf.org.uk
Provides information, advice and support for men experiencing difficulties with child access or who are finding it difficult to come to terms with limited child access.

International Stress Management Association (UK)
Department of Psychology
South Bank University
103 Borough Road
London SE1 OAA.
www.isma.org.uk
Tel: 07000 780430
Provides information, advice and details of stress management practitioners and trainers.

MIND
Granta House
15-19 Broadway
Stratford
London E15 4BQ
Tel: 020 8519 2122
Mind Information Line 0845 766 0163
www.mind.org.uk
Advice and information service on mental health problems.

National Council for One Parent Families
255 Kentish Town Road
London NW5 2LX

Tel: 020 7428 5400
Helpline: 0800 018 5026 Calls are free & confidential.
www.oneparentfamilies.org.uk
Offers information, advice and support on a range of issues affecting one parent families.

National Phobic Society
Zion Community Resource Centre
339 Stretton Road
Hulme
Manchester M15 4ZY
Tel: 0870 7700 456
Website: www.phobics-society.org.uk/
User-led organisation, run by sufferers and ex-sufferers of anxiety disorders supported by a high-profile medical advisory panel

No Panic
93 Brands Farm Way
Telford
Shropshire TF3 2JQ
Tel (office): 01952 590005
Helpline: 01952 590545
Web: www.no-panic.co.uk
Help for people with panic attacks, phobias and obsessive-compulsive disorders

Open Door Association
447 Pensby Road
Heswall
Wirral
Merseyside
LR1 9PQ

Tel: 0151 443 0183
Help for those with agoraphobia

Pax (incorporating Agoraphobia Information Service)
4 Manorbrook
London SE3 9AW
Web: www.panicattacks.co.uk
Information and advisory service for people who experience panic attacks, phobias and anxiety.

Phobic Action
Greater London House
547-551 High Road
London E11 4PB
Tel: 0208 558 6012 (helpline)
Tel: 0208 558 3463 (office)
Provides information, advice and counselling to those whose lives are affected by a phobia.

Relate
Herbert Gray College
Little Church Street
Rugby
Warwickshire CV21 3AP
Tel: 0870 601 2121
www.relate.org.uk
Provides counselling for couples.

Relaxation for Living
29 Burwood Park Road
Walton-on-Thames
Surrey KT12 5LH
Tel: 01932 227826

www.relaxationforliving.co.uk
Courses and information on how to deal with stress.

Release
388 Old Street
London EC1V 9LT
Tel: 020 7928 1211
Helpline: 020 7729-9904
www.release.org.uk
Provides advice and information on drug misuse.

SAD Association
PO Box 989
Steyning
West Sussex BN44 3HG
Tel: 01903 814942
Web: www.sada.org.uk
Information, newsletter and support for Seasonal
Affective Disorder.

Social Anxiety Disorders Sufferers (SAD)
Web: http://www.social-anxiety.org.uk/
SAD provides support and information for Social Anxiety
Disorder sufferers in the UK. The site is maintained by
volunteers who themselves have experienced SAD. The
aims of SAD include providing sufferers with current,
valid, and useful information on the condition, either
directly or through links; providing a starting point for
finding help in overcoming SAD and offering members a
way of communicating with each other.

Samaritans
10 The Grove
Slough

Berkshire
Tel: 01753 532713 or 0345 90 90 90
www.befrienders.org
Telephone counselling and drop-in centres.

Triumph Over Phobia (TOP UK)
PO Box 1831
Bath BA2 4YW
Tel: 01225 330353
Web: www.triumphoverphobia.com
Structured self-help groups to help with recognizable phobia and obsessive–compulsive disorder. Send SAE for information.

UKRC (United Kingdom Register of Counsellors)
1 Regent Place
Rugby
Warwickshire CV21 2PJ
Tel: 0870 443 5232
www.bacp.co.uk
Register of counsellors in the UK

UKCP (United Kingdom Council for Psychotherapy)
167 Great Portland Street
London W1N 5FB
Tel: 0207 436 3002
www.psychotherapy.org.uk
Register of psychotherapists in the UK

Victim Support
Cranmer House
39 Brixton Road
London SW9 1DZ
Tel: 0207 735 9166

www.victimsupport.com
Offers information, advice, counselling, and support to those who have been the victims of crime. Local branches.

This book
Thoughts form (pp. 41–42)
Relaxation exercises (pp. 19–22 and pp. 75–77)
Responsibility pie (p. 46–47)

CONTACT ME

I am keen to know if my books are of help to readers and in what ways I can improve the information provided. If you would like to comment you can e-mail me at gladeana@dircon.co.uk or you can send a letter to me via the publishers of this book.

INDEX

adrenaline (*see also* stress
    hormones), 4, 22, 55,
    69, 75, 85, 123
anchoring, 21, 78, 85
anxiety, 1–4, 6–9, 12–13,
    15–19, 21–22, 26–27,
    29, 31–32, 42, 48–49,
    51–52, 54–55, 60,
    66–69, 73, 76, 80, 82,
    84–87, 93, 97, 108, 111,
    128–130, 137–139
-free actions, 72, 80
-free diet, 123–127
-free life, 64, 114
-free thinking, 41, 72–73
assertion/assertiveness/
    non-assertiveness, 71–72,
    95–113, 118
    broken record, 103–104
    criticism, 111–112
    deflection, 105
    discrepancy, 106
    negative feelings, 104
    put-downs, 112–113
    rights and responsibilities,
        106–107

'thinking it over' time, 106
    three steps to, 102–103,
        118–119
    workable compromise,
        104–105

'big I, little i', 44–45, 57,
    70
body language, 65
breathing, 4, 19–20, 75–78,
    81, 85, 93–94

cognitive–behavioural therapy
    (CBT)/therapist 1–3, 32,
    132
coping imagery, 77–79,
    84–86
coping strategies, 9, 18, 78,
    80–81, 84–86
core beliefs, 50–52, 70
    three-stage model of,
        52–53
cortisol (*see also* stress
    hormones), 4
cost–benefit analysis, 70–71,
    91

counselling/counsellor(s), 1,
129, 132–135, 138,
140–142

demands and challenging
them, 48–51
depression, 2, 6, 8, 49, 87,
124
diet and anxiety, 22, 58, 87,
123–126
distraction techniques, 59
dreams/nightmares, 25

emotional intelligence,
60–61, 67
strong emotions,
66–67
exercise, 68–69

faulty thinking, 31–32
form, 41–42
fears list, 78, 84–85
fight or flight, 4, 6
food; *see* diet and anxiety
freeze response, 5

generalized anxiety disorder
(GAD), 6, 12
graded exposure, 80–82
guilt, 69–70

healthy thinking, 32
help
psychotherapy, 129
reading, 130
resources, 131–141 *see also*:
medication

self-help groups, 128
talking, 128
hyperventilation, 20, 76–77
hypochondriasis, 12–13

life audit, 57–59
life beliefs/rules, 30–31,
47–48, 52
life-saver exercise, 75–76
liking/respecting yourself,
53–57, 64

medication, 17, 86, 129
anti-depressants, 87
monoamine oxidase
inhibitors (MAOIs),
87
benzodiazepines, 86
tranquillisers, 86
mental illness, 16

National Health Service
(NHS), 2
National Institute for Clinical
Excellence (NICE), 2
negative thinking, 33–48
negative automatic
thoughts (NATs), 33
nervous breakdown, 16
noradrenaline (*see also* stress
hormones), 4

obsessive compulsive disorder
(OCD), 6, 12–13, 137
Office for National Statistics
(ONS), 6
optimism/optimistic, 27–29

panic
   attack(s), 14–15, 77,
      82–84, 137–13
   disorder, 6, 14–15
pessimism/pessimistic, 9,
      27–28
phobias, 6, 14, 128–129,
      137–138, 140
   social, 14
post traumatic stress disorder
      (PTSD), 13
problem-solving, 87–95
   brainstorming, 90–91
   continuum, 94
   managing setbacks, 92
   personal contingency plan,
      93
   post-it notes, 93–94
   six-stage model, 88
   SMART technique, 89–90,
      94
procrastination, 67–68
psychotherapy/
      psychotherapist(s), 1,
      129, 132–133, 140

rational emotive behaviour
      therapy (REBT), 52,
      131
relaxation, 18–20, 24, 75,
      128, 138, 141
responsibility pie, 45, 47, 70,
      141
Robinson's Four Stages of
      Learning (to change),
      26–27

shame and humiliation, 7, 49,
      72–73
sleep, 7, 12, 23–25, 116
   rapid eye movement
      (REM), 23
   sleeping tablets, 86
stress/stressful, 8–9, 15,
      18–19, 22–23, 49, 53,
      83, 120–122, 133,
      135–136, 139
   and exercise, 69
   burn-out, 15
   busting, 120, 123
   hormones, 4, 15–16, 123
   management, 18 58, 122,
      133, 136
   response, 4–6, 12, 15, 31,
      55
   scale of, 121
   symptoms, 10, 15
support systems/networks/
      organizations, 8, 10, 18,
      55–56, 120, 131–141

time management, 7,
      22,114–117, 120
   diaries and organizers, 119
   filing systems, 119
   post-it notes, 119
   time allocation pie, 116
   'to do' lists, 119

visualization, 20, 75, 77–79,
      91–92

worry, 73–75